It was good enough for Buddha,
Plato, Socrates,
Hippocrates, Ovid,
Aristotle, Shelley,
Tolstoy,
George Bernard Shaw . . .

Here's news about food combining for better health . . . mythmaking and the protein-diet controversy . . . all about fasting . . . minerals, vitamins, supplements . . . meat vs. other proteins . . . and two food value tables precisely measuring the elements of nearly 500 common foods. . . .

Learn why vegetarian foods may be the best thing
to happen to YOUR diet—and to your life!

PROTEIN
FOR
VEGETARIANS

GARY and STEVE NULL and STAFF

PYRAMID BOOKS • NEW YORK

All tables in this book are from
the United States Bureau of Statistics.

PROTEIN FOR VEGETARIANS

A PYRAMID BOOK

First printing February, 1974

Copyright © 1974 by Gary Null
All Rights Reserved

ISBN: 0-515-03307-3

Printed in the United States of America

Pyramid Books are published by Pyramid Communications, Inc. Its trademarks, consisting of the word "Pyramid" and the portrayal of a pyramid, are registered in the United States Patent Office.

PYRAMID COMMUNICATIONS, INC.
919 Third Avenue
New York, New York 10022, U.S.A.

As with all books completed by Gary and Steve Null and the staff of the Nutrition Institute of America, every effort is taken to minimize contradictions and errors, and to present as definitive and complete a work as can be prepared for the subject matter being written.

The following staff members prepared the material for *Protein for Vegetarians*:

James Dawson
Chief Editor, N.I.A.

Richard Bull
Assistant Editor

Steve Null
Research Director

Diana Powers
Librarian for New York Public Library
Research Assistant

Jerry Krutman
Research Editor

Ollie Black, Rajah Afghan, and Edith Stern
Contributing Editors

ACKNOWLEDGMENTS

The following list of names is by no means complete. Rather, their research on the subjects of protein and vegetarianism was of particular value in the preparation of this book:

J. I. Rodale	Hereward Carrington, Ph. D.
Herbert M. Shelton	Barbara Davis
Bob Hoffman	Frances M. Lappe
R. F. Milton	Ellen Buchmanewald
F. Wokes	A. M. Altchul

For more detailed reading concerning the topics of food combining, fasting, and protein, we refer the reader to *The Complete Handbook of Nutrition* by Gary and Steve Null and Staff, published by Robert Speller and Sons, 10 East 23rd Street, New York, New York, 10010.

The tendency of writers on nutrition has been either to make their books so technical that the lay reader would find the book difficult to comprehend, or so general as to offer only a broad introduction. The purpose of each book in the series by Gary and Steve Null and Staff is to fill the gap between these two extremes by providing basic information to the lay reader in a step by step progression, gradually increasing the reader's knowledge of nutrition.

The *Complete Handbook of Nutrition* was the basic primer with capsulated observations on many of the more important areas of health and nutrition. We have followed this with separate books dealing in a comprehensive manner with important categories, i.e. *Food Combining Handbook, Body Pollution, Herbs for the 70's,* etc. *Protein for Vegetarians* is our latest effort in the ongoing series.

Due to our desire to have each book complement the best information of the preceding one, some of the information in every book is repeated from the preceding ones.

We feel that overlapping important facts will assist the reader in learning step by step, in a pyramidal way.

Gary and Steve Null
New York City
November, 1973

TABLE OF CONTENTS

CHAPTER ONE

VEGETARIANISM

"More and more, in the next thirty years, we are going to be resorting to a vegetarian diet," Dr. Isaac Asimov predicted on a recent television talk show. The reasons for this, he explained, are not moral or humanitarian, but because plants remain our healthiest, largest, and most economical source of food. The noted writer and biochemist is not alone in making such a prediction.

A commission of the National Academy of Science in the United States has come to a similar conclusion. To survive in the future, the commission reported, we will all have to rely more on plant foods for sources of protein, instead of the traditional American diet of meat.

Ecologist Jarvis Eldrid of West Virginia University warned a meeting of nutritionists at Morgantown, West Virginia: "The day when man can wantonly prey upon the diminishing species with whom he shares this planet is nearly over. Let us hope the lengthening shadows are not specters of doom."

Vegetarianism is not new. It has been long established in India as an integral part of the Hindu religion. Plato and Socrates were vegetarians, as were Hippocrates, Ovid, Aristotle, and Buddha.

British poet and vegetarian Percy Shelley insisted in 1813 that, "Man's digestive system was suited only to plant food." Fifty years later, British dramatist George Bernard Shaw wrote, "A man of my spiritual intensity does not eat corpses." On a lighter note, Russian novelist Leo Tolstoy said, "Feeding upon the carcass of a slain animal has something of a bad taste about it."

Vegetarianism has been misunderstood throughout most of history. Its practitioners have been called faddists, fanatics and mystics. There was seemingly something odd about a person who didn't eat meat. Hitler's vegetarianism, for example, has often been noted as one of his quirks. Even the word itself is widely misunderstood.

Etymologically, vegetarian does not come from 'vegetable,' but rather from the Latin word *vegetare*, which means "to enliven." When the Romans used the term *homo vegetus*, they referred to a vigorous person, sound in mind and body. Yet people today think of a vegetarian only as a vegetable eater!

The range of vegetarian diets is wide, almost as wide as the reasons people adhere to them. Some vegetarians eliminate meats from their diets, but continue to eat fish, poultry and dairy products; others eliminate meat and a combination of these foods. And many, of course, will eat only plant food. It would be unfair to say any one of these groups represents the 'true' vegetarian.

The reasons people give for being vegetarians are many. A few base it upon their religious beliefs, others claim health benefits. Most, however, came to vegetarianism out of rational judgment. It is this last reason which will primarily concern us in this book. We feel that vegetarianism is a rational alternative to the meat-centered American diet.

THE NEED FOR A RATIONAL ALTERNATIVE TO THE AMERICAN DIET

One of the strongest reasons for taking a serious look at our diet and seeking alternative menus is the proliferation of processed foods in this country over the past few years. The extensive processing of our foods causes many nutritional problems. While there is little chance a person living in America will starve to death, there does exist the danger of malnutrition.

Nutritionists like Adelle Davis are beginning to make us aware of the large gap between good health and the absence of illness. Most of us in this country fall into the gray area between these two categories. Unfortunately, Americans are *not* the world's best-fed people.

The title of a book published several years ago sums up two of the problems of the American diet: *Overfed and Undernourished*. Both overeating and undernourishment are detrimental to health, like overexertion and inactivity. In our case the two are paradoxically related.

We Americans consume large quantities of food but much of it is processed and gives us only naked calories. Therefore, the average person may have to eat three times as much food as he really needs to keep his system operating at peak performance. This excess causes many of us to suffer poor health.

Meat, of course, is one of the highest sources of proteins available, and Americans eat plenty of it. But few people realize that protein, vitamin B12, phosphorus, potassium, and magnesium are practically its only nutrients. Plants provide more than twice the amount of vitamins and minerals as meat. Meat is high in both phosphorus and potassium, but many vegetables and dairy products are higher. Cheddar cheese is twice as high in phosphorus, and baked potatoes and lima beans are 30 to 50 percent higher. Also, the magnesium content of vegetables is much higher than meat.

With the exception of vitamin B12, you can get all your vital nutrients from vegetable and fruit sources. B12 can be obtained from dairy products and eggs.

The nutrients of meat are not enough by themselves to keep you healthy and at peak efficiency. The same is true of other single foods. If you concentrate your diet on any one type of food, you'll suffer from a lack

13

of certain elements. Only the foods containing a variety of essential elements are sufficient to sustain life. A vegetarian diet *will* provide all of these necessary elements.

Let's take a look at these elements. They include protein, fats, carbohydrates, mineral salts and vitamins, all of which humans obtain from food to replace worn-out body tissue.

The processes which keep us alive are those that wear out tissue. As the tissue is broken down the wastes are eliminated and the tissue itself replenished by the foods we eat. On the average the body remains at approximately the same weight. The complex nature of these tissues demands we replace the proper elements.

If only one essential element is missing from your diet, your health will suffer. This was dramatically illustrated in an experiment carried out by Harold Rossiter and Charlotte Beckner at Woodburn College in Pennsylvania. They put ten dogs on a diet primarily of fats, and all ten of them became round and plump. All died.

The absence of a single nutrient may cause pellagra, niacin deficiency, rickets, vitamin deficiency, scurvy, and beri-beri. You need every nutrient to obtain and maintain optimum health.

Although protein cannot singly maintain our diets, it is the most important element. It is probably also the most misunderstood. Many people mistakenly believe that a meat-centered diet is the only possible diet which supplies all the proteins and other nutrients your system needs. One rational alternative is to concentrate on getting all or most of your essential nutrients from plant sources.

Protein supplies most of the muscle-forming elements your body requires and acts as a fuel for energy. This second function can be as important as the first. About

14

half of the protein you take into your body is transformed by the liver into the sugar, glucose. This process plays an important role in maintaining your energy level. You need fats and carbohydrates to supply heat and energy to your system and to influence protein metabolism. Vitamins and minerals are absolutely essential in keeping your metabolism working correctly.

How well your bodies are supplied with these essential elements and to what extent your systems use them have a profound effect on your life. Nutrition might not make you ambitious but it can supply you with the energy to fulfill your ambitions. Poor nutrition can rob you of the energy you need to do the things you want. Recent research has shown that what you eat can even influence your mood and your psychological and emotional well being. *You Are What You Eat!*

REASONS FOR CUTTING DOWN
MEAT CONSUMPTION

Can you get too much protein? There are many people who insist that you cannot. Recent evidence, however, shows that for some people a high protein diet might actually be harmful. This evidence falls into two categories.

Nutritionists argue that eating too much protein is a potential health hazard because of the toxic substances created by the presence of more protein in your system than you can use. Eating too many fats or carbohydrates can cause an excess that is not immediately dangerous. Proteins, on the other hand, immediately create uric acid and a variety of toxic substances which can poison and devitalize your system. An excess of carbohydrates will produce fermentation. An excess of protein results in putrefaction.

Another argument against a high protein diet is the

discovery by Dr. George Watson, during research which lead to his book *Nutrition and Your Mind*, that some people have trouble oxidizing the substances taken into their bodies to produce energy. Proteins are oxidized at a slower rate than carbohydrates and fats, and if such a person has a heavy protein diet, he is compounding the problem and not getting enough energy to operate at a maximum level.

This brings up the very important point that the same diet is not necessarily adequate for everyone. A diet which meets all the needs of one person and allows him to operate at peak level of health may cause just the opposite effect in someone else. We've all heard of cases of individuals living to be very old on eccentric diets; but the reason for their reaching old age might not be the diet per se, but rather their particular metabolic make-up.

The old adage "One man's meat is another man's poison," is quite literally true. It is important that diet information be applied to oneself and patterned on one's own particular needs.

UNFIT FOR HUMAN CONSUMPTION

Meat is a complete protein, one of five different types of complete protein. Meat could be a good source of protein if it were not for the many toxic chemicals which are used so heavily by most meat producers. Aside from the high quality of protein, meat also contains decaying cell nuclei. The cell tissues of cattle contain several forms of naturally occurring poisons which are generally thrown off through the process of elimination. However, it is impossible for the animal to throw off all of the accumulated toxins. If the animal were unable to eliminate the majority of these toxins it would die of selfpoisoning. It is important to understand that along with the usable protein in meat you are also getting these biological waste by-products.

Toxins manufactured within the animal are not the only poisons which we're concerned with. Just as some of the pesticides you use end up stored in your bodies, and you have every right to be concerned about this, so do some of the pesticides taken in by animals get stored in their bodies and pass on to you when you eat their meat. A large portion of the poisons and pesticides you consume comes from the meat you eat. Taking a close look at the sources of pesticide residues in the United States diet, you'll see that you take in 0.281 parts per million of DDT, DDE, TDE pesticide residues through meat, fish, and poultry. You take in only 0.112 parts per million from dairy products. And in order of decreasing amounts: 0.041 ppm from oils, fats, and shortenings; 0.036 ppm from leafy vegetables; 0.027 from fruits; 0.026 ppm from legumes; 0.008 ppm from grains and cereals; 0.007 from root vegetables; and 0.003 from potatoes.

There is a wide gap between the amount of pesticides you receive from meat, fish and fowl, and the amount taken in from the next lowest category, dairy products: a 0.169 ppm difference. In other words, meat, fish and fowl contain more than twice as many parts per million residue of pesticides than does the second highest category. The next highest sources of pesticide residues are oils, fats, and shortenings, which measure 0.041 ppm. Again, this is less than half of the next highest category.

By eliminating meat, fish and fowl from the diet and replacing these items with other forms of complete protein, you can reduce the amount of pesticide residue in your food supply by half. Of course you will have to consume twice the amount of plant protein to equal the reduction of animal protein in your diet.

In addition to pesticides, meat contains several other

17

unhealthy additives. You would never sit down to a meal and order a plate of methoxychlor, chlordane, heptachlor, toxaphene, lindance, benzene, hexachloride, aldrin, dieldrin, with a side dish of DDT and garnished with pesticides. Or try an unappetizing plate of stilbestrol, aureomycin, mineral oil residue and a dozen other chemicals, all added to beef and stored in the fatty parts of meat. Regrettably, this is exactly what you would find in a piece of roast beef.

Of course most people enjoy their roast beef with gravy. Even the gravy will contain DDT and several other pesticides, in addition to antibiotics and toxins created by the interaction between the chlorine-dioxide bleach used on the flour and the flour nutrients.

THE CHEMICAL BARRAGE

It is a harrowing truth that today few animals in your meat supply escape the barrage of chemicals that, while they do not produce sudden death, poison your bodies. Can anyone insist that these chemicals are not likely to lead to chronic illness and slow deterioration of your bodies? Residues of these chemicals are passed on to every meat eating consumer. No other article in the American diet is as thoroughly tampered with as the meat you eat.

The average steer is conceived by artificial insemination. He is raised on an artificial sex-hormone implanted in his ear, fed with synthetic hormones, antibiotics, and insecticides, and shot with tranquilizers. He grazes on pastureland contaminated by radioactive fallout and pesticides. After spending his life on this chemical feast, he is then slaughtered for your table, offering the primary source of protein in the American diet. Not a very reassuring picture, is it?

The farm, where nature once had a balance, has become a factory geared to the chemical alteration of nature. No matter how disillusioning this might be to the romantics, the point is that these chemicals are being passed on to you in the food you eat. And it is unlikely that the picture is going to change drastically in the near future.

According to the June 1968 issue of *The Farm Journal*, still further chemical alteration might be in store for you. *The Journal* told the farmers that researchers are forcing activated charcoal down the throats of cows in order to trap some of the pesticide residues. The idea behind this is similar to using charcoal filters on cigarettes to trap the tars resulting from the burning of tobacco. This solution to pesticides in meat seems a little ridiculous, analogous to giving everybody a gas mask with activated charcoal filters to breathe polluted air instead of doing something about cleaning up the air in the first place.

The researchers do not stop there. These cows will also be fortified with treatments of the enzyme-stimulating drug, phenobarbital, which is available from any veterinarian by prescription.

Drugs are also used to slow down the cattle's metabolism so they'll put on more weight from less food. Up to 90 percent of all cattle going to market each year have received artificial hormones. But they are not alone. It is an accepted practice in the United States to feed antibiotics and tranquilizers to all our meat animals. One hundred million chickens are receiving these hormones. An antibiotic dip has been used to increase the shelf life of chickens and turkeys. And the Food and Drug Administration has recently given milk farmers permission to feed their cattle antibiotics.

It would be reassuring to know farmers were not allowed to add anything to beef cattle, chickens, or dairy cows which is hazardous to health. But this is simply not the case, as can be illustrated by the story of stilbestrol.

19

Stilbestrol is an artificial female sex hormone which farmers use for the simple economic reason that a few pennies worth of the hormone planted in a cow's ear results in an extra twelve dollars worth of beef. If this chemical is mixed with their feed, cattle gain weight 15 percent faster on 12 percent less feed. Stilbestrol is said to be worth 675,000,000 pounds of beef annually.

To date scientists can't explain exactly how weight is increased in beef or chickens with the female sex hormone stilbestrol. The Food and Drug Administration believes stilbestrol may affect the glandular system to cause the weight increase. In those animals where stilbestrol was used, "hypertrophy" (excessive development) of the liver, adrenal glands, and pituitary gland was noted.

There have been several outspoken critics of stilbestrol. One is Dr. Robert K. Enders, chairman of the department of Zoology at Swarthmore College. He is also an unsalaried advisor to the United States Department of Agriculture and the Department of the Interior. Dr. Enders admits that the use of stilbestrol makes the food more attractive but, referring specifically to its use in chickens, warns that "the use of the drug to fatten poultry is an economic fraud. Chicken feed is saved, but it is merely turned into fat instead of protein. . . . This fat is of very doubtful value and is in no way the dietary equal to the protein that the consumer thinks he is paying for." Not only has a chemical been added to your diet by using stilbestrol in chickens, but the chemical has lowered the quality of the product you buy. It raises the fat content and correspondingly lowers the protein content of the chicken. This would be bad enough, but there's more. Stilbestrol has been shown to be a health hazard. Among the many pathogenic conditions caused by stilbestrol are excessive menstrual bleeding, cysts and cancers of the uterus, arrested growth of children, fibroids of the uterus,

20

breast pain in women, premenstrual tension, cancers of the cervix, breast and uterus and leukemia and tumors of the sexual glands in animals. Stilbestrol in men can cause impotency and sterility.

When stilbestrol was first tested in the early 50's on a group of volunteer women, no harmful results to their health were detected. Twenty years later the women were still in good health, but their daughters had developed vaginal cancer during adolescence. This test makes a strong case for those who question the long range effect of chemicals added to your food.

MORE CHEMICALS IN MEAT

The chemical feast forced on the livestock you eat does not stop at the farm. The list of chemicals commonly used in curing and preserving cold meats is a long one. And all these added chemicals are poisons.

Sodium nitrate and sodium nitrite are common in luncheon meats. They have both recently been shown to be cancer-causing agents. One of the reasons these chemicals are used is because they accentuate the natural color of the food, making it more appealing and costlier. Both chemicals have been known to poison meat consumers.

One example of the inability to control the amounts of nitrites in meats was the several cases of illness in New Orleans, caused from frankfurters supposed to contain no more than 200 parts per million of nitrites. However, upon inspection the frankfurters actually contained up to 6,650 ppm of nitrites.

Before using any food which contains any amount of boric acid you should know that the Food and Drug Administration considers it "poisonous per se". Yet there have been reported cases of boric acid being "dusted on hams during the curing process" to keep off a fly infection.

One of the most infamous of the surreptitious chemicals is sodium sulphite, a substance both dangerous and illegal. It is frequently used in manufacturing certain foodstuffs. The same is true of sodium benzoate.

John Cullen, a former Canadian food-inspection official, has warned,

> If the meat is of an unusually red color, it is reasonable to assume that it has been doped and doctored with sulphurous acid or sodium sulphite. This is especially true in the case of hamburger that has been made from stale meat trimmings, pork kidneys, pig's hearts, sheep hearts and other meat by-products including large quantities of fat. [These chemicals are a] great favorite with butchers and manufacturers of meat products generally. This preservative is very dangerous to health, especially when used in meat, because it will not only restore the color of putrid and almost black meat, but also because it will destroy the strong odor of putrefaction.

But this is not the end of Mr. Cullen's story. He goes on to say that

> many butchers will contend that they use this preparation only because it arrests the spread of bacteria. Nothing, however, is further from the truth. Changes of the most dangerous character are continuously taking place in the meat, but sodium sulphite obscures them and makes the meat appear to be fresh and of better value than it really is, and enables the seller to perpetrate an unscrupulous and deliberate fraud.

Chemical additives can be very dangerous, but they are not the only consideration vegetarians take into account when explaining their case against meat as the mainstay of their diets. This is the hygienic argument we touched on earlier.

If a person were to watch cattle being slaughtered and prepared for sale, it would probably have some effect on his desire to eat meat. A little insight into the internal cell changes once the cattle are slaughtered should prove even more interesting.

Death is not immediate to a slaughtered animal. In fact, for several hours after the slaughter the tissues will be consuming the soluble food-material still in the blood stream. The hygienic problems occur during these hours between the time the animal loses consciousness and the time all cell activity ceases. While the animal was alive those toxic by-products of elimination were quickly removed from the system through the lungs, liver, kidneys, and other excretory organs. Harm results when the waste causes the destruction of tissues and cells, after the somatic (bodily) death. The flesh of an animal carcass is loaded with toxic blood and other waste by-products. Cooking, aging or chemical additives can not extract from or lessen the effects of these poisons on the animal.

For the reader who is concerned about the extent of the adulteration of our total food supply, including meat, we refer you to *Body Pollution*, by Gary and Steve Null and Staff, published by Arco.

MEAT VERSUS OTHER SOURCES OF PROTEIN

The only important nutritional element we derive from meat is protein and its related substances. Meat lacks all other food factors essential to good health.

There are other sources of protein that contain these other essential nutrients. Not only do they have a high percentage of protein, but in some cases they are a more economical supply of this important substance. Some of these foods are beans, peas, lentils, eggs, cheese, whole grains, and especially nuts. The two highest protein nuts are cashews and almonds. Nuts are not only rich in protein, but also high in other important substances, mostly minerals.

One important argument against the place of meat in the national diet is the fact that much of the food which could be a direct source of protein to Americans is instead fed to cattle to produce meat protein and little else.

Livestock have the ability to convert inedible and low-quality material into high quality food for human consumption, but this potential is not exploited as much as it should be, especially in industrial countries like the United States. Enormous quantities of the *highest* quality food sources are fed to animals, instead. In this country one half of our harvested agricultural land is planted with feed crops. In fact, *we feed 78 percent of all our grain to animals.*

The high-quality food we feed to livestock is wasted. Cattle, sheep, and goats do not need to eat protein in order to produce protein. Micro-organisms in their stomachs can convert nitrogen in the form of urea into protein. The absurdity of feeding cattle very nutritious grains which humans could better use and afford can be seen by the Department of Agriculture statistics for 1970. Grazing cattle were fed approximately twenty-three million tons of high quality protein, which produced only one million tons of beef protein. In effect, cattle raisers wasted twenty million tons of high quality grains which could have been used by humans.

Table 1. Protein Supplies (1963-65) (per capita) and per day—by regions and subregions

Regions and Subregions	Calories	Animal Proteins	Vegetable Proteins	Total Proteins
FAR EAST (incl. China Mainland)				
South Asia	2,050	8.6	46.2	54.8
Southern Asia Mainland	2,020	6.4	43.0	49.4
Eastern Asia	2,180	13.1	36.3	49.4
Southern Eastern Asia Major Islands	2,350	20.5	54.6	75.1
China Mainland	2,040	7.1	33.6	40.7
	2,010	8.2	50.5	58.7
NEAR AND MIDDLE EAST	2,410	14.0	57.6	71.6
AFRICA	2,170	10.9	47.6	58.5
North Africa	2,100	10.9	44.1	55.0
West and Central Africa	2,120	7.8	46.9	54.7
East and Southern Africa	2,270	15.0	49.8	64.8
LATIN AMERICA	2,590	24.1	43.5	67.6
Brazil	2,780	19.4	49.4	68.8
Mexico and Central America	2,500	21.3	45.0	66.3
Northern and Western countries of South America	2,220	22.2	36.3	58.5
River Plate Countries	3,090	50.5	37.0	87.5
DEVELOPING REGIONS	2,140	10.7	46.9	57.6
EUROPE (incl. U.S.S.R.)	3,050	42.8	44.8	87.6
Eastern Europe	3,180	32.4	56.7	89.1
Western Europe	3,020	45.4	41.9	87.3
NORTH AMERICA	3,140	65.3	27.8	93.1
OCEANIA	3,230	63.9	31.5	95.4
DEVELOPED REGIONS	3,070	48.3	40.8	89.1
WORLD	2,380	21.0	45.1	66.1

25

Table 2. Percentage contribution of various commodities to percentage supplies (Protein supplies 1963-65)

	Cereals	Starchy roots and tubers	Pulses nuts and seeds	Vegetables and fruits	Vegetable proteins	Meat	Eggs	Fish	Milk	Animal proteins
FAR EAST (incl. China Mainland)	59.3	3.3	18.0	3.3	84.3	6.6	0.7	4.6	3.8	15.7
South Asia	64.5	1.0	19.6	4.0	87.1	1.4	0.2	1.4	9.9	12.9
Southern Asia Mainland	58.8	2.0	8.3	4.0	73.5	7.1	1.4	15.4	2.6	26.5
Eastern Asia	48.2	2.1	14.0	8.4	72.7	6.1	2.9	15.6	2.7	27.3
South Eastern Asia Major Islands	64.4	6.4	7.4	3.9	82.6	7.1	1.0	8.6	0.7	17.4
China Mainland	57.8	4.6	20.3	3.2	86.1	10.0	0.5	2.7	0.5	13.9
NEAR AND MIDDLE EAST	67.8	1.0	6.7	4.9	80.1	8.0	0.7	1.4	9.5	19.6
AFRICA	54.7	9.1	15.7	1.9	81.4	9.2	0.5	4.1	4.8	18.6
North Africa	69.9	1.1	5.1	4.2	80.3	7.8	0.8	1.6	9.5	19.7
West and Central Africa	51.2	14.8	18.1	1.6	85.7	6.8	0.4	5.1	2.0	14.3
East and Southern Africa	55.1	4.5	15.6	1.7	76.9	12.5	0.6	3.4	6.6	23.1
LATIN AMERICA	39.8	4.0	16.9	3.4	64.3	18.3	1.9	2.7	12.7	35.7
Brazil	37.9	3.6	26.6	3.7	71.8	13.5	2.2	2.3	10.2	28.2
Mexico and Central America	44.3	2.1	18.2	3.0	67.9	12.7	1.8	2.4	14.9	32.1
Northern and Western Countries of South America	41.0	7.5	8.5	4.3	61.8	18.8	1.2	4.8	13.2	38.2
River Plate Countries	32.7	4.2	2.5	2.9	42.3	41.0	2.1	1.4	13.0	57.7
DEVELOPING REGIONS	57.2	3.8	16.8	3.3	81.4	8.3	0.9	4.0	5.4	18.6
EUROPE (incl. U.S.S.R.)	36.8	5.5	3.8	5.4	51.5	21.5	3.8	4.2	18.8	48.5
Eastern Europe	50.0	6.4	3.0	4.2	63.6	16.4	2.5	1.5	15.1	36.4
Western Europe	33.5	5.4	3.9	5.6	48.4	22.8	4.1	4.9	19.8	51.6
NORTH AMERICA	17.6	2.6	4.6	5.2	30.1	36.3	5.8	2.9	24.9	69.9
OCEANIA	24.9	2.4	2.2	3.6	33.1	36.8	4.2	3.1	22.5	66.9
DEVELOPED REGIONS	31.9	4.7	3.9	5.3	45.8	25.4	4.3	3.9	20.4	54.2
WORLD	47.9	4.1	12.1	3.9	68.2	14.7	2.1	3.9	10.9	31.8

LAND FOR MEAT OR LAND FOR PEOPLE?

In the United States it is hard to believe we'll ever have a shortage of food. The same is not true of the rest of the world, unfortunately, and might not be true, as Dr. Asimov pointed out, even in America by 2001.

The rising cost of meat seems to be like the weather: everybody complains, but nobody does anything about it. Just on the basis of how much plant protein goes into one pound of meat protein, the cost of one pound of meat protein is twenty times higher than one pound of plant protein, without taking into account the added cost of manhours and equipment needed to get that one ton of meat protein.

If we take one acre of land to produce food, the choice of how we are going to use that land will be determined by several factors. One of them should be how much food we can get from that one acre by using it in different ways. If we're concerned with producing protein for our own consumption or for the consumption of a group, we have several choices. We can use the land for meat production, cattle grazing or feed growing for meat animals. However, if we use that acre for cereal production we'll produce five times more protein for consumption. An acre planted with spinach will give us twenty-six times the amount of protein we would have if we devoted that acre to meat production.

Many authorities feel that we place too much emphasis on meat in our diets and should give more attention to the importance of vegetables, legumes, dairy products and grains. In fact, it has been estimated that 35–45 percent of the world's livestock is fed grains from which we could benefit nutritionally. If we conserved our grain supply and gave it to the poor and malnourished, instead of to cattle, we could easily feed

27

nearly all of the chronically underfed people in the world.

Since we use between one-third and one-half of the continental land surface of the world for grazing and 40 percent of this land in producing vegetable sources suitable for human consumption, we can see that 15 to 20 percent of the continental land surface could be converted to producing food directly available for human use. The lands which produce vegetable sources of protein used for grazing could be turned into an inexpensive source of protein food if people relied less on meat and more on plant sources.

An unshaking emphasis on producing meat as the backbone of the American diet not only uses up vegetable sources of protein, but also other sources of food. In 1968 up to one-half of the world's fish catch was fed to livestock.

BUT ISN'T MEAT NECESSARY?

There are many people who consider plant protein inferior on two counts. First they assume meat to be the highest, richest, and most easily obtained source of protein. Secondly they believe that vegetable protein is inferior in quality and hardly worthy of human consumption.

Is meat actually the richest source of protein? Not necessarily. There are plants which rank higher than meat in the quantity of protein they provide, particularly in their processed form. *Soybean flour, for example, is over 40 percent protein, while meat is rarely more than 20 to 30 percent protein.* Some cheeses are also very high in protein. Parmesan cheese, for instance, is 36 percent protein. Meat, as a source of protein, ranks lower than these two sources, ranging from 20 to 30 percent protein, which is not much higher than dried beans, peas, and lentils. These three are essentially in the same range as meat, with 20 to 25 percent protein.

What about the quality of the protein you get from plants? This quality can be measured scientifically and computed into figures, called the Net Protein Utilization, or NPU. We will cover this term more closely in the next chapter.

The NPU lets you know what percentage of the protein you eat is actually available to your bodies, and is a good measure of the protein quality of your diets. The scale of foods in terms of Net Protein Utilization, based on a United Nations publication, ranges from 40 to 94.

The highest NPUs are 94 percent for eggs and 83–89 percent for milk. Although meat protein is represented for its quality and quantity of protein, it is not at the top of the list. Soybeans and brown rice and some cheeses are high in their NPUs.

In one aspect, animal proteins are superior to plant proteins because they more nearly match the requirements of the human body. This does not mean, however, that you must use meat as your main source of protein, because dairy products also contain these animal proteins. The only advantage of this protein is that you need to eat less meat than plants to fulfill your essential amino acid requirements.

But you have seen that plant sources of protein are many times more plentiful than meat sources on this planet, and that it is not necessary to rely fully on meat. You can get your supply of proteins from other sources. How this is done will be examined in the following chapters.

SUMMARY

There are several reasons behind the increasing popularity of vegetarian diets. Many of them are based on rational judgments rather than moral, religious, or faddist claims.

From the purely practical point of view, any area of land will supply more vegetable protein than meat protein. In many cases, the soil given to feeding cattle could supply twenty times more plant protein for human consumption if this land was devoted to grains and fruits and nuts.

It is possible to derive high quality sources of protein from plants. The protein deficiencies of one plant are easily covered by the richness of another. The amount of varied proteins you take in from plant sources can be sufficient to fill your needs.

By obtaining your proteins from a plant source instead of animal sources, you can reduce the amount of toxins taken into your body, which in turn should help reduce illness and possibly lengthen life.

There are some common sense rules to follow when eating a vegetarian diet, but most of them apply to any diet:

Chew thoroughly, especially when eating nuts.

Do not eat when you are excessively tired, excited or worried. Such states can interfere with your digestive system.

Take a few minutes to rest before each meal so that your body can handle the food better. You should not exercise after eating.

Finally, do not think more food is required under a vegetarian diet.

A de-emphasis on meat can be a rational alternative to the American diet, if you are rational in applying it. The information in the following chapters should equip you with an understanding of your needs, especially for protein, and the facts about a vegetarian diet.

The next step is to take a close look at how your body handles proteins, how much protein you need and why, and what the best sources of proteins are. We will also discuss the combination in which foods can be eaten for proper digestion, assimilation, utilization, and elimination.

Chapter Two

UNDERSTANDING PROTEINS

It would be hard to overestimate the importance of protein in your diet. One of the most significant facts about protein is that it is the major substance which supplies you with the materials of which your body is made. Protein is the most abundant substance in your body. You are 18 to 20% protein by weight. Your muscles, skin, hair, nails, eyes, teeth, blood, heart, lungs, brain and nerves are mostly protein.

A third of the body's protein is in muscles. A fifth is in bones and cartilages, a tenth in the skin, and the remainder in the other cell tissues and body fluids.

Your bile and urine do not contain any protein at all. Only proteins contain nitrogen, sulfur, and phosphorus, which are all essential. Protein must first be converted into starch or sugar, and once converted it cannot be changed back into protein, no matter how badly it is needed. While vitamins and minerals are essential to good health, and starches and sugars are essential as fuel, you need the building blocks of protein to keep you alive. Increasing age often requires an increased intake of protein for the body to be well nourished. If you are deficient in your protein intake, you are in effect lowering your resistance to infection or disease. This is important as you get older and cannot utilize proteins as well. Proteins also assist in the exchange of nutrients between cells and intercellular fluids, and between tissues and the blood and lymph.

You also rely upon proteins for the myriad reactions involved in metabolism, the process that keeps your body running. This metabolic process is regulated by special proteins (hormones) and catalyzed by other proteins (enzymes).

All foods contain carbon, oxygen, and hydrogen. You derive these substances from starches, sugars, fats, and proteins.

There are hundreds of different proteins; all the basic ones come from other animals and plants. Since your body cannot store proteins, it needs a continuous supply. When you take in protein your body will use what it needs at that moment and turn the rest into fuel to be used when energy is needed.

You need a continuous supply of protein because the cells are constantly breaking down and being replaced. Every cell replaces itself within approximately 160 days. Vital organs change more quickly. The liver regenerates every two weeks. Since these organs are made up of proteins, only proteins can be used to build, repair, or maintain your body.

The amount of protein you need is dependent on many factors. Age is important—people past forty-five need more protein than younger people. Their ability to digest and assimilate proteins has fallen off. An older person cannot utilize his protein intake as completely as a youth, and if he continues to take in the same amount of protein as he always has, even if that amount had been sufficient in his younger days, he will suffer from a deficiency.

Another major factor that determines protein need is lifestyle. If you are under severe stress your protein needs increase quickly. During times of stress or illness as much as 135 grams of body protein can be destroyed in one day. Therefore, adjust your protein intake to your lifestyle. Your body can not synthesize the "non-essential amino acids" rapidly enough to meet a sudden demand for protein because of stress or illness. By keeping track of your daily intake of protein

33

you can easily adjust it to protect yourself. During a mild illness you should increase your protein intake to 80–120 grams a day.

There are many types of proteins in your blood. One of these is called hemoglobin. Hemoglobin transports oxygen from the lungs to the tissues of the body and brings back carbon dioxide to the lungs to be eliminated from the body. Almost 95 percent of the hemoglobin molecule is protein (the other 5 percent is iron).

There are other proteins in the blood which give the human body the means to resist certain viruses and infections. Gamma globulin, another blood protein, also forms antibodies which can neutralize bacteria and viruses and other harmful micro-organisms.

Proteins are instrumental in maintaining the fluid balance throughout the system. When the body is too low in protein, this fluid balance becomes upset.

All proteins in the body are in a constant state of exchange. Molecules or parts of molecules of protein are constantly breaking down, while other molecules and parts of molecules are being built up as replacements. This exchange is characteristic to all life processes. Continuous turnover of cells and molecules explains why your diet must supply an adequate amount of daily protein even after you no longer need it for growth. The rate of protein turnover is faster within the cells of the tissue, called intracellular, than in the substance between the cells, which is called intercellular.

PROTEIN AND BLOOD SUGAR

The basic source of fuel for all the organs of the body is blood sugar (glucose). Our understanding of the relationship between the level of blood sugar and the food we eat is a relatively recent discovery. The brain and nervous system depend upon this sugar to function properly.

Cellular respiration is the process by which complex foods are broken down into simpler substances. These substances are then oxidized in the individual cells. We think of oxidation as a burning process, but glucose is actually transformed through a series of compound stages by the action of enzyme proteins. Each step of this process is interlocked with the other. As these compounds are broken down, then built back up again, different amounts of energy are formed at different stages to provide the energy needs of the body.

Packets of energy are called *adenosine triphosphate* or ATP. *Glycolysis* and the *citric acid cycle* refer to the energy cycles in which these packets are released and produce Pyruvate (energy) and O-acetate, respectively.

Impaired mental functioning can result if these conversion cycles of glucose are disturbed. A great number of reactions, each depending on the previous reaction in step by step fashion, determine whether or not these packets of ATP are released.

Brain metabolism can be placed in serious jeopardy whenever the energy cycle is interrupted at points where enzymes should be released. Enzymes are proteins in another form. The nervous system depends upon sufficient amounts of niacin (vitamin B3) and other vitamins and minerals. The kinds and quantities of fuel required by the tissues in the body effect the ability of the nervous system to transform glucose into energy.

The rate at which a system oxidizes foods is the determining factor in how much energy becomes available to that system. Dr. George Watson, in *Nutrition and Your Mind*, classifies patients as slow oxidizers, fast oxidizers, and suboxidizers. Different diets are required by each of these groups to function efficiently. Using the diets of people in a group other than yours would be harmful to your body. Because of these findings it is most important that a qualified physician determine which diet is proper for you.

Protein is a source of sugar protein, which produces pyruvate (energy), and fat protein, which produces acetate. When proteins are converted into the simpler substances, they are called amino acids. Both acetate and pyruvate are necessary for the production of energy.

Proteins also contain another class of substances called *nucleoprotein,* which greatly influences the energy-producing quotient of the tissues. Nucleoproteins are conjugated with nucleic acids and aid the energy mechanism of cells. A purine base nucleoprotein called adenine is the most important of this group.

A constituent of ATP, the principle energy carrier of the cells, adenine is also part of the complex intermediate, acetate, from which is derived most of the energy you utilize.

The body can synthesize adenine from CO_2, aspartic acid, glutamin, formate and glycine; but it is important for it to be obtained through your diet as well. Nucleoproteins which are obtained from food are necessary to prevent you from becoming anxiety-ridden. These natural substances mark the difference between a well-functioning and an ineffectively functioning nervous system. Fish and animal products are the richest sources for purine content, but your system can be maintained at peak efficiency from vegetables which give you from 50 to 150 milligrams per 100 grams of food. Among the vegetables in this category are:

asparagus	peanuts
beans	peas
cauliflower	spinach
lentils	whole-grain grains and cereals
mushrooms	yeast

Your metabolic type notwithstanding, sufficient amounts of varying kinds of protein are necessary to your diet. Blood glucose provides the only source of energy which the brain and nervous system must have to survive.

Carbohydrates (starches and sugars) and protein directly maintain this essential blood sugar level. The quantity of fat being burned in the tissues affects the blood sugar level indirectly.

All the carbohydrates you ingest are changed into glucose, while only half of your protein intake can be transformed in this way. Glucose, like proteins, cannot be stored for later use. The average person cannot store more than a four-hour supply of this blood sugar, which provides the body's main source of energy.

Some of the proteins which contribute to maintaining the blood sugar level work through the liver, where most of the body's sugar is stored. At this stage the sugar is called glycogen, or "liver sugar." Gluconeogenesis is the process through which energy-producing protein is first transformed into glycogen and then into glucose.

This is the way the body maintains the level of blood sugar. After eating a properly-balanced meal, the carbohydrates are digested first, then converted into glucose. The blood stream carries part of this glucose to the tissues to be used as fuel, and some of the remainder is stored in the liver as glycogen.

The digestion of protein is a much slower process. The protein can be transformed into glycogen gradually and then stored in the liver until future needs require that it be released into the blood stream.

As the supply of blood sugar from the carbohydrates is exhausted, the glucose manufactured from the protein can then be drawn upon. Of course, this reserve source of glucose will not exist unless your diet contains enough carbohydrates in addition to the necessary amount of protein.

This interaction between proteins and carbohydrates maintains the level of your blood sugar. Without a balanced supply of both proteins and carbohydrates, neither can function efficiently. Protein will be changed into liver sugar or blood sugar only when the body burns up the sugar already available in the blood.

Without the proper amount of protein being ingested, the supply of blood sugar provided by carbohydrates will be used within a few hours, and the body will not be able to draw glucose from the liver. When this happens, the level of blood sugar drops.

HOW DOES YOUR BODY USE PROTEINS?

Protein has, as one of its functions, the ability to produce energy, but it has other important jobs to perform. In order for protein to be able to do this additional work, other substances must be taken into the body to help meet energy needs. Therefore, a balanced intake of oils, fats and carbohydrates is necessary to allow the protein in your system to function in these other areas.

Amino acids are the chemical units which proteins become soon after digestion. The biological and nutritive value of your protein supply is determined by amino acids. A lot of different kinds of protein are broken down into relatively few amino acids. It is the proportion of these different kinds of amino acids that determines their nutritive value to your body.

Of the twenty-two amino acids that exist, your body can synthesize fourteen of them. The remaining eight amino acids, which are called "essential," cannot be synthesized. Therefore, your body must depend entirely on your food supply for these eight essential amino acids.

When you eat the proper assortment of amino-acid-producing proteins and the proper amount of them, you get the most nutritional value possible. When a protein includes the eight essential amino acids, we call it a "complete" protein, since that substance provides all of the amino acids which the body cannot manufacture without protein.

The next step in the digestive process is the separation of these amino acids into their basic elements: carbon, hydrogen, oxygen, and nitrogen. When this is complete, these elements are carried through the blood stream to the liver and then dispersed to all parts of the body.

On their way to the necessary areas, the amino acids are reassembled into special combinations of "manufactured" proteins. These new, synthesized proteins replace dead cells and help in tissue growth, or create enzymes, hormones and other active compounds.

Since there is no way for the body to store amino acids, those which are not fully used are returned to the liver. There a process, known as deaminization, takes place. During deaminization, the building process is reversed, causing the amino acids to revert to their elemental state. The carbon, oxygen and hydrogen fragments are used to provide energy as the body needs it. The excess nitrogen is passed through the urine as urea.

THE BALANCE BETWEEN ACID AND ALKALI

Protein also helps maintain the body's balance between the acid and alkaline state. Parotid glands assist the digestion of protein when the acid–alkaline balance is upset. The digestion and assimilation of all classes of protein are almost stopped if the parotid glands are dehydrated.

Alkalinity and Acid

Alkalinity is necessary to the life process. Seeds will not germinate unless first softened and alkalinized by water. Conception cannot occur if a mother's cells are not alkalinized. This process falls under the Law of Polarity—the earth and all contained therein is a manifestation of the fusion of positive and negative forces, with a line of balance in the center. In the body there must be a balance between alkali and acid.

The pituitary gland seems to be the balancer in the event of alkaline-acid imbalance, while the other glands have subsidiary duties.

Other activities of the pituitary gland include: regulating fluid intake and output, stimulating lactation and the thyroid gland, and sexual development. The pituitary gland is also involved in the stimulation of growth and of metabolism (digestion and assimilation). It starts the menstrual cycle and helps steady gaseous metabolism.

An imbalance in the acid–alkaline content occurs when one eats food of such poor quality that the subsidiary glands become overtaxed and congested. When this happens the entire body mechanism is thrown off track. Disappointment, shock, or emotional upset should never unbalance a properly-nourished person.

One of the chief functions of the thyroid gland is to prevent the body from absorbing the toxic wastes from proteins. To achieve this, the thyroid employs iodine. With its alkaline basis, iodine has the power to neutralize acid. Animal proteins contain a high quantity of toxic matter, and the ingestion of too much of these proteins might well cause a thyroid imbalance. That is not to say that excluding animal proteins from the diet is the simple solution. Too much of any one food can be harmful. The knowledge of both the quantity of protein a person must have to replace tissue, supply heat, and maintain blood sugar level and the capacity to handle protein is important.

A person's individual make-up determines the amount of a given food he can handle. Proper digestion and assimilation can make the difference between health and illness.

The largest gland in the body is the *liver*. While it stimulates peristalsis, the major function of the liver is to secrete the bile which assists digestion in the intestines.

The wave-like contractions along the alimentary tract, which force its contents onward, are described by the term *peristalsis*. Another necessary function of the liver, with the help of the spleen, is to break down dead blood cells and continuously detoxify the blood.

The *pancreas gland* releases a digestive fluid containing ferments, which break down all classes of food. The chief function of this six-inch organ is the secretion of insulin to regulate fat and sugar metabolism. The pancreas is also a detoxicator.

The *suprarenal glands* provide immunity against infection while attending to the healing of cuts and wounds.

The *kidneys,* like the alimentary tract, the skin, and the lungs, are chiefly concerned with excretion. All the excretory processes are stimulated by the suprarenals. Their energizing qualities affect mental, emotional and physical well-being.

As the body's defender, the kidneys can separate iron tablets, animal hormones, pep drugs, undigested proteins, and other harmful substance in the fluid of the body and eliminate them through the urine. The urine of a healthy person is 95% water. Also present in urine are inorganic salts and organic waste material including urea, creatinine and uric acids. Over-accumulation of these harmful substances can result in permanent body damage.

Toxemia, a dispersement of toxins (poisonous substances) throughout the body, will deplete the suprarenals quite rapidly. This condition allows easy detection of any imbalance of these glands. Muscular weakness, hot flashes and sudden chills from a circulatory origin, dryness of the mouth, nervous tension, a sense of overall weakness, and a fall in blood sugar are all symptoms of glandular imbalance.

The *parotid glands* and the *salivary glands* are two lesser known glands located in front of each ear. The parotids are the largest of the mucous glands. The salivary glands produce the fluids necessary for digestion. Saliva, the colorless fluid produced by the combined secretions of these glands, contains digestive ferments and enzymes. One of these ferments, ptyalin, changes starch into dextrin and sugar.

Rapid loss of the body's acid–alkaline balance occurs when the paratids fail to secrete at the same time the digestive glands in the stomach are unable to produce hydrochloric acid in sufficient quantities to change proteins into amino acids. This condition is called alkalosis or increased alkalinity of the body fluids. Acidosis is excessive acidity and, since most people are far too quick to judge this to be the cause of their trouble, alkalosis is the more difficult to overcome. Antacids worsen alkalosis.

It is difficult to know whether the parotids or the pituitary has the most influence over the sex organs, because this is an area in which the two function parallel with each other.

Let's now examine the parotid gland and its relationship to the common symptoms of acid–alkaline imbalance. Since a negative and a positive force form every chemical compound, parotid secretions, which are alkaline and therefore negative, would not be able to function without gastric acids, which are positive.

The body can get only the percentage of nourish-

42

ment which the parotids are secreting of their normal quota. Distress would not be produced under a low percentage of functional capabilities, but there would be deterioration of muscle and other tissues. However, decreased peristaltic action and near paralysis of the bowels results from deficiencies of liver fluids. Stagnation and decay of undigested food in the intestines is a greater problem of parotid disturbance than slow starvation.

Just as nature produces moss to sweeten a stagnant pool of water, the body creates a fungus to absorb the decaying waste matter which accumulates in the organs. This fungus is a protective organism which attaches itself to part of the body—the ears, eyes, liver, tonsils, heart, mastoids—where accumulations of toxic waste threaten to destroy the cells. Having done its work, the fungus disappears.

The *parathyroid glands*, located behind the thyroid gland, have as their major function the task of keeping calcium in the bloodstream. Normally four in number, these small glands also destroy waste products, especially protein by-products which affect the nervous system.

Whenever the parotids and suprarenals are out of commission, the parathyroids take over the depleted glands' functions until they become active and back in balance.

Acid: Keynote of Energy

Working together, acids and alkalies are an integral part of the life process. Alkalies hold back the driving force of the positive acids. Without acids, cells would stop recreating new cells and your body would quickly decline. Conversely, without alkalies, the stomach would digest itself, and the unchecked acids would burn up the body.

The pituitary gland directs activities during the constant state of flux which accompanies the re-creation of cells. This busy organ is thrown off balance after any shock hits the system, be the experience heavy exercise, quick temperature change, mental stress, or even a meal. Time out for reestablishing that balance is a must for this overworked organ. Several hours generally pass before a state of near balance is reached.

Heartburn, certain gastric conditions, and arthritis, among others, are the symptoms of acid–alkaline imbalance, but do not necessarily mean that you are suffering from acidosis. They could possibly be warning you of alkalosis. Never prescribe for or diagnose yourself. Your family doctor can spare you pain and lingering illnesses, so don't make matters worse for him.

TYPES OF PROTEIN NEEDED BY YOUR BODY

We have discussed how a sufficient supply of protein every day is necessary for continued physical and emotional health, but what kinds of proteins are needed by the body?

In the past it has been thought that a certain quantity of any of the tremendous variety of proteins would keep you healthy, but recent research takes a new look at this subject. Not only are all eight essential amino acids needed to be present at the same time, but you must get them in the right proportion. Dr. Roger Williams of the University of Texas has discovered that the proportion of nutrients is more critical than the quantities in many cases. This is particularly evident in developing vitamin formulas for people under stress and those with problems concerning alcohol.

In summary, here are the three crucial factors concerning proteins in the diet.
1. Of the twenty-two necessary amino acids, there are eight which the body cannot manufacture and must be obtained from outside sources. These are called "essential" amino acids.

2. All eight of these essential amino acids must be present in the system at the same time.
3. All of these eight must be present in the right proportions.

This last factor is the most critical if you want to pursue a vegetarian diet. Most of the food proteins you eat contain all the eight essential amino acids. However, in some plant sources one or more of the eight are usually present in a disproportionately small amount.

These amino acids present in a small amount are called "limiting amino acids." Their name is appropriate because they limit the use of all the seven other protein components.

The "limiting amino acid," which determines the utilization of all the essential amino acids, reduces the effectiveness of those amino acids ingested. A protein food which contains enough tryptophan to satisfy 100 percent of the utilizable pattern's requirement and 100 percent of the necessary leucine level but only 50 percent of the needed lysine, has no greater value to your system than a food which contains only 50 percent of all the essential amino acids.

Only one pattern of the essential amino acids can be used by the body. If all the essential amino acids aren't present in the proper proportion, you can use them only to the extent that the "limiting amino acid" allows you to. As soon as the protein reaches the cell, the "assembling center" in the cell will release the extra amino acids which cannot be used above the level of the limiting amino acid. The remainder is then used by the body as fuel.

The "biological value" of any given protein food is the percentage of absorbed protein your body actually uses. Much of the protein you take into your system is lost in the digestive process, according to the pattern your body follows.

Then there is the Net Protein Utilization factor, which tells how much of the protein you eat is actually available to your body. The NPU of a food is determined by how closely the essential amino acids in its protein match the body's own utilization pattern. The amino acid pattern of egg protein most closely matches this ideal pattern.

HOW MUCH PROTEIN YOU NEED

Understanding the facts of protein nutrition is of the utmost importance before experimenting with a new diet.

There are three separate considerations which determine the proper protein allowance for different people.

1. You must determine your minimum need.
2. You must make allowances for your individual differences.
3. You must make an adjustment for protein quality.

The major disagreements among nutritionists are over the first consideration: determining the body's minimum need for protein. But even here the differences are not so great as to make meaningless some kind of average.

YOUR MINIMUM PROTEIN REQUIREMENT

By measuring the amount of nitrogen secreted in the urine of people on protein restricted diets, scientists can determine how much protein your body is using. The reason for this is that nitrogen is the characteristic component of protein and not found in fats or carbohydrates. This test will show how much protein your body is using up to satisfy your body requirements, but this figure may vary greatly depending upon the amount of exercise, general health of the person, rate of meta-

46

bolism, conditions of stress, and other individual characteristics.

There are many formulas for the suggested minimum daily requirement of protein. Therefore, an individual must consider his own unique situation when deciding his protein needs. We strongly suggest that one add to his diet more protein than the minimal requirement as a safety factor.

An additional adjustment should be made to allow for the possible ingestion of low-quality protein. By referring to our explanations of the differences in quality among proteins, one can easily adjust his diet accordingly.

CHAPTER THREE

UNDERSTANDING FOOD VALUES

This chapter is intended to aid the reader in the practical application of the information presented so far.

The emphasis is placed upon unprocessed and "minimally" processed foods, since they are generally higher in protein and other nutrients than processed food.

The foods are listed in descending value of usable protein within each category. For each food you are given both the total grams of protein for an average serving and the number of usable grams of protein the food provides.

Seafood

Many people on a vegetarian diet will include seafood in their diets. Fish is close to meat in protein content and often superior in protein quality. It is also particularly high in the amino acid lysine.

Fish has been a successful staple diet for many people, especially in the Orient. Since rice is deficient in lysine and isoleucine, fish makes an excellent supplement to it.

SEAFOOD

Average Serving, 3½ oz or about 100 grams	Total Protein	Usable Protein
1. Tuna, canned in oil, drained	24 grams	19 grams
2. Mackerel, Pacific	22	18
3. Halibut	21	17
4. Humpback salmon	20	16

Average Serving, 3½ oz or about 100 grams	Total Protein	Usable Protein
5. Swordfish	19	15
6. Striped bass	19	15
7. Rockfish	19	15
8. Shad	19	15
9. Shrimp	19	15
10. Sardines, Atlantic, in oil	21	14
11. Carp	18	14
12. Catfish	18	14
13. Cod	18	14
14. Pacific herring	18	14
15. Haddock	18	14
16. Crab	17	14
17. Northern Lobster	17	14
18. Squid	16	13
19. Scallops, 2 or 3	15	12
20. Flounder or Sole	15	12
21. Clams, 4 large, 9 small	14	11
22. Oysters, 2 to 4	11	9

Dairy Products

Milk is only 4 percent protein. Eggs are only 13 percent protein. But these figures are misleading. You will remember from the protein quality discussion earlier that both of these foods contain the highest quality protein. The Net Protein Utilization (NPU) of milk is over 80 percent, and that of eggs is a startling 94 percent. Your body can use almost all of the protein it takes in from these two sources. Two cups of milk will supply more than one-third of your daily protein allowance.

The NPU range of dairy products is from 70 to 94. Most of them fall between 70 and 83. Dairy products are also high in calcium, so if dairy products are eliminated from your diet you should find another source of calcium.

Like fish, dairy products are very high in lycine.

49

Consuming them can help you make up for lysine's deficiency in plant protein sources. But some dairy products are not good sources of protein. Cream, sour cream, and cream cheese contain too many calories for the protein they have. Butter contains no protein at all.

NUTRITIVE VALUE OF EGGS

Dietetic characteristic	Amounts per 100 g (excluding shell)		
	Units	Yolk	White
Water	g	49	87.8
Ash	g	2.0	0.3
Crude protein	g	16.0	10.9
Gross energy	g	347	50.9
Carbohydrate	g	0.6	0.8
Fats: Total	g	30.6	0.2
sat. fatty acids	g	10.3	—
oleic acid	g	14.7	—
linoleic acid	g	2.5	—
Calcium	mg	141	9.0
Phosphorus	mg	569	15
Iron	mg	5.5	1.1
Sodium	mg	52	146
Potassium	mg	98	139
Thiamine	μg	224	4.4
Riboflavin	μg	440	271
Niacin	μg	44	110
Vitamin A	i.u.	3,400	0

Calculated from original data of Brooks and Taylor (1955) and Watt and Merrill (1963)

DAIRY PRODUCTS

Average Serving	Total Protein	Usable Protein
1. Cottage cheese, 6 tbsp.		
creamed	14 grams	11 grams
uncreamed	17	13
2. Egg white, dried,		
or powdered ½ oz.	11	9

Average Serving	Total Protein	Usable Protein
3. Milk, nonfat dry solids, tbsp. 1 oz.	10 grams	8 grams
4. Parmesan cheese, 1 oz.	10	7
5. Milk, slim, whole or buttermilk, 1 cup	9	7
6. Yogurt from skim milk, 1 cup	8	7
7. Swiss cheese, 1 oz.	8	6
8. Edam cheese, 1 oz.	8	6
9. Egg, 1 medium	6	5
10. Ricotta cheese, ¼ cup	7	5
11. Cheddar cheese, 1 oz.	7	5
12. Roquefort cheese or blue mold, 1 oz.	6 5	4 4
13. Camembert cheese, 1 oz.	5	4
14. Ice cream, about ⅕ pint	5	4

Legumes (Dried Peas, Beans, and Lentils)

Many people overlook the important role of legumes in a vegetarian diet because they think of them as being dull, but some legumes actually have a protein content equal to or greater than that of meat.

Soups can be made from lentils, peas, black beans, and soybeans. It takes only a little imagination to turn these foods into a part of your daily diet.

All legumes are at least 20 percent protein. The highest, soybeans and mung beans, have NPU's of 61 and 57 percent, respectively.

LEGUMES

Average Serving, ¼–⅓ cup dry	Total Protein	Usable Protein
1. Soybeans or soy grits	17 grams	10 grams
2. Mung beans	12	7
3. Broad beans	13	6

Average Serving, ¼–⅓ cup dry	Total Protein	Usable Protein
4. Peas	12 grams	6 grams
5. Black beans	12	5
6. Cowpeas (blackeye)	12	5
7. Kidney beans	12	5
8. Chickpeas	11	5
9. Lima beans	10	5
10. Tofu (Soybean curd), wet, 3½ oz.	8	5
11. Lentils	13	4
12. Other common beans	11	4

Nuts and Seeds

Nuts and seeds are as rich in protein as the legumes and their Net Protein Utilization (NPU) factor is often higher. Nuts are seldom given a place of any importance in the American diet, yet they contain important minerals. The Brazil nut, for instance, is important in a vegetarian diet because of its sulfur-containing amino acids which are rare in plant protein. Nuts are also a good source of fat essential in maintaining good health.

Some nuts are not considered good sources of protein because of the high ratio of calories to protein. These include pecans, chestnuts, coconuts, filberts, hazelnuts, macadamia nuts, almonds, pine nuts, and English walnuts.

Nuts and seeds tend to be high in tryptophan and sulfur, but they are generally deficient in isoleucine and lysine.

The following is a compositional breakdown of some nuts.

CHEMICAL COMPOSITION OF NUTS
AND DRIED FRUITS

NUTS	Water	Pro-tein.	Carbo-hydrate	Fat	Min-erals
Acorns	4.10	8.10	48.00	37.40	2.40
Almonds	4.90	21.40	16.80	54.40	2.50
Beechnuts	9.90	21.70	19.20	42.50	3.86
Brazil nuts	4.70	17.40	5.70	65.00	3.30
Butternuts	4.50	27.90	3.40	61.20	3.00
Candlenuts	5.90	21.40	4.90	61.70	3.30
Chestnuts (dried)	5.90	10.70	74.20	7.00	2.20
Chufa	2.20	3.50	60.70	31.60	2.00
Coconut	14.10	5.70	27.90	50.60	1.70
Filberts	5.40	16.50	11.70	64.00	2.40
Hickory nuts	3.70	15.40	11.40	67.40	2.10
Paradise nuts	2.30	22.20	10.20	62.60	2.70
Pecans	3.40	12.10	8.50	70.70	1.60
Pignons	3.40	14.60	17.30	61.90	2.90
Pignolias	6.20	33.90	7.90	48.20	3.80
Pistachios	4.20	22.60	15.60	54.56	3.10
Black Walnuts	2.50	27.60	11.70	56.30	1.90
English Walnuts	2.50	18.40	13.00	64.40	1.70
Water Chestnuts	12.30	4.00	50.00	1.20	1.77
Peanuts	7.40	29.80	14.70	43.50	2.25
Peanut Butter	2.10	29.30	17.10	46.50	2.20
Almond Butter	2.20	21.70	11.60	61.50	3.00
DRIED FRUITS					
Apples	26.10	1.60	62.00	2.20	2.00
Apricots	29.40	4.70	62.50	1.00	2.40
Pears	16.50	2.80	66.00	5.40	2.40
Peaches	20.00	3.15	50.00	.45	2.15
Prunes	22.30	2.10	71.20	—	2.30
Raisins	14.60	2.60	73.60	3.30	3.40
Currants	17.20	2.40	74.20	1.70	4.50

Average Serving, 1 oz.	Total Protein	Usable Protein
1. Pignolia nuts 2½ tbsp.	9 grams	5 grams
2. Pumpkin and squash seeds	8	5
3. Sunflower seeds (3 tbsp.) or meal (4 tbsp.)	7	4
4. Peanuts	8	3
5. Peanut butter	8	3
6. Cashews	5	3
7. Sesame seed (3 tbsp.) or or meal (4 tbsp.)	5	3
8. Pistachio nuts	5	3
9. Black walnuts	6	3
10. Brazil nuts	4	2

The size of the servings here are conservative. One ounce of peanuts will supply only 7 to 8 percent of your daily protein needs. A 10-cent bag of peanuts (about 1½ ounces) gives 10 to 12 percent.

Grain Cereals and Their Products

Cereals are not considered a source of protein in the United States, but they provide almost half the protein in the world's diet. Their percentage of protein content is not high.

As with other sources of protein, grains and cereals must be evaluated from two different aspects—the quantity and quality of the protein they provide.

There are wide differences in the quantity of protein among various grains. Wheat, rye, and oats, for example, have 30 to 35 percent more protein by weight than rice, corn, barley, and millet. Not only does the protein content vary from grain to grain, but it varies within one type of grain. Wheat can range from 9 to 14 percent protein. The wheat with the highest protein content is hard red spring wheat. Durum wheat, often used in pasta, has the second highest protein content at 13 percent.

NPU values of cereal range from the low 50s to the low 60s. There are some exceptions, however. Whole rice has a NPU of 70 percent, the same as meat. Next is whole wheat germ with an NPU of 67 percent. Oatmeal and buckwheat have NPU values of 66 and 65 percent. All these values are higher than most other vegetable protein sources and comparable to beef.

Many of the grains and cereals are deficient in isoleucine and lysine. Foods rich in these essential amino acids should be added to your diet.

GRAINS, CEREALS, AND THEIR PRODUCTS

Average Servings		Total Protein		Usable Protein	
1. Wheat, whole grain hard red spring, 1/3 cup	8	grams	5	grams
2. Rye, whole grain 1/3 cup	7		4	
3. Egg noodles, cooked 1 cup	7		4	
4. Bulgur (parboiled wheat), 1/3 cup, or cracked wheat cereal 1/3 c.	6		4	
5. Barley, pot or scotch, 1/3 c.	6		4	
6. Millet, 1/3 c.	6		3	
7. Spaghetti or macaroni cooked 1 c.	5		3	
8. Oatmeal, 1/3 c.	4		3	
9. Rice, 1/3 c.				
a. brown	5		3	
b. parboiled (converted)	5		3	
c. Milled, polished	4		2	
10. Wheat germ, commercial 2 level tbsp.	3		2	
11. Bread, commercial 1 slice, whole wheat or rye	2.4		1.2	
12. Wheat bran, crude 2 rounded tbsp.	1.6		0.9	

One Cup of Flour	Total Protein	Usable Protein
1. Soybean flour, defatted	65 grams	40 grams
2. Gluten flour	85	23
3. Peanut flour, defatted	48	21
4. Soybean flour, full fat	26	16
5. Whole wheat flour or cracked wheat cereal	16	10
6. Rye flour, dark	16	9
7. Buckwheat flour, dark	12	8
8. Oatmeal	11	7
9. Barley flour	11	7
10. Cornmeal, whole ground	10	5
11. Wheat bran, crude	9	5

Except for soybean flour, all of these flours are deficient in isoleucine and lysine and should be complemented by other protein sources. Legumes are the ideal match for grains since they are high in these amino acids. Brewer's yeast is also an excellent complement.

Remember, it is not only important to get enough protein, but to get it in the right proportions. The safest way to assure this is to eat different sources of protein.

Vegetables

Vegetables are not going to make a large contribution to your protein needs, but they contain many vitamins and minerals essential for good health and vitality. Most of the vegetables listed here are low in calories so you need not be concerned about eating too many of them.

Vegetables high in vitamins and minerals include: snap beans, beets, burdock, cabbage, eggplant, lettuce, onions, green peppers, pumpkins, radishes, rhubarb, squash, sweet potatoes, tomatoes, and turnips.

Many of the vegetables listed as sources of protein are deficient in sulfur content and isoleucine and should be complemented by sesame seeds and Brazil nuts. Millet, parboiled rice, and mushrooms are also high in sulfur content.

The average serving of vegetables here is based on a fresh, uncooked weight of 3½ ounces.

VEGETABLES

Average Serving, 3½ oz.*	Total Protein	Usable Protein
1. Lima beans, green	8 grams	4 grams
2. Soybean sprouts	6	3
3. Peas, green, shelled	6	3
4. Brussels sprouts	5	3
5. Corn, 1 med. ear	4	3
6. Broccoli, 1 stalk	4	2–3
7. Kale, stems, cooked	4	2
8. Collards, cooked	4	2
9. Mushrooms	3	2
10. Asparagus	3	1.8
11. Artichoke	3	1.8
12. Cauliflower	3	1.8
13. Spinach	3	1.5
14. Turnip greens, cooked	3	1.4
15. Mung bean sprouts	4	1.4
16. Mustard greens	3	1.4
17. Potato, white, baked	2	1.2
18. Okra	2	1.2
19. Chard	2	1

*Average serving: based on fresh, uncooked weight.

Dried Fruits

The most important value of dried fruits is their content of carbohydrates and mineral matter. In order to maintain optimum health, one must have fats and fluid substances, vitamins, and carbohydrates.

Carbohydrates form the bulk of the food most people eat: breads, potatoes, vegetables, fruits, and some nuts. There are three types of carbohydrates—sugar, starch, and cellulose (gums and pectins).

The sugar content of dried fruit is far greater than of fresh fruit, but you should eat both. Fruits contain vitamins, juices, and acids. Dried fruits are rich in minerals, and only sea foods such as clams, lobsters, and oysters can compare with them. The minerals found in dried fruits are potassium, sodium, calcium, magnesium, iron, sulphur, silicone, and chlorine.

See Table page 53.

Nutritional Additives

The main purpose of nutritional additives is to boost your protein intake. A small amount of powdered egg white or "tiger's milk" can give your diet a substantial protein boost. One teaspoon of the former or ¼ cup of the latter can fill 12 to 25 percent of your daily protein requirement.

NUTRITIONAL ADDITIVES

Average Serving	Total Protein	Usable Protein
1. Egg white, powder, ½ oz.	11 grams	9 grams
2. Tiger's milk, ¼ cup	7	5
3. Brewer's yeast, powder, 1 level tbsp.	4	2
4. Wheat germ, commercial, 2 level tbsp.	3	2

Except for tiger's milk, these additives are all especially high in lysine, the amino acid that is most often missing from plant sources of protein.

VITAL ELEMENTS IN COMMON FOODS

There are, of course, many other vital elements that your body needs besides proteins.

One of the important vitamins a vegetarian lacks in his diet is B12, which others normally get from meat. Adelle Davis recommends that vegetarians supplement their diets by taking 50-microgram B12 tablets once a week to prevent a deficiency in that vitamin.

The following is a listing of the vital elements found in common foods:

CALCIUM
    Cheese (American)
    Milk (whole)
    Cheese (cottage)
    Milk (butter)
    Cauliflower
    Broccoli
    Endive
    Celery
    Beans
    Rutabagas
    Spinach
    Turnips
    Carrots
    Molasses
    Oysters
    String beans
    Cabbage
    Lettuce
    Eggs
    Nuts
    Citrus fruits
    Maple syrup
    Dried fruits
    Dried beans

CARBON
    Potatoes
    Brown Sugar
    Whole Wheat
    Shredded Wheat
    Honey
CHLORINE
    Oysters
    Cheese
    Lettuce
    Whey
    Cabbage
    Parsnips
    Beets
    Turnips
    Milk
    Watercress
    Fish
    Celery
    Cottage cheese
    Dates
    Dandelion
    Coconut
    Carrots
    Tomatoes

Bananas
Pineapple
Grapes
Lemons

FLUORINE
Cauliflower
Cod liver oil
Goat's milk
Egg Yolk
Cheese
Brussels sprouts
Milk
Garlic
Sauerkraut
Sea Food
Rye Bread
Cabbage
Whole Grains
Spinach
Watercress
Beets

HYDROGEN
Vegetables
Fruits
Milk
Water

IODINE
Lobster
Clams
Oysters
Shrimp
Blue Fish
Mackerel
Haddock
Cod
Scallops
Halibut

Salmon
Squash
Radishes
Asparagus
Lettuce
Milk
Cabbage
Cucumber
String Beans
Spinach
Beets
Potato
Kelp
Sea Lettuce

IRON
Beans
Egg Yolk
Peas
Wheat
Oatmeal
Prunes
Spinach
Parsley
Kale
Cheese
Potato
Chard
Watercress
Oysters
Dates
Raisins
Beets
Figs
Oranges
Mushrooms
Turnips
Tomatoes

Bananas
Carrots
MAGNESIUM
Cocoa
Chocolate
Almonds
Cashews
Peanuts
Lima Beans
Whole Wheat
Brown Rice
Oatmeal
Dates
Raisins
Chard
Spinach
MANGANESE
Pineapple
Wheat
Navy Beans
Blueberries
Walnuts
Kidney Beans
Beets
Lima Beans
Gooseberries
Spinach
Peaches, dry
Blackberries
Apples
Apricots
Beet greens
Cabbage
Beets
Wheat Bran
Bananas
Watercress

Carrots
Celery
Lettuce
NITROGEN
Peas
Lentils
Mushrooms
Cheese
Nuts
Fish
Lima Beans
PHOSPHORUS
Lima Beans
American Cheese
Oatmeal
Fish
Eggs
Spinach
Buttermilk
Milk
Almonds
Grapes
Lentils
Pecans
Brown Rice
Walnuts
Whole Wheat
Brussels Sprouts
Corn
Dandelion
Lobster
Peas
Soybeans
POTASSIUM
Cabbage
Coconut
Figs

Tomatoes
Apricots
Peaches
Onions
Lima Beans
Pineapple
Milk
Prunes
Pears
String Beans
Eggplant
Celery
Watercress
Raisins
Cauliflower
Potatoes
Parsley
Citrus Fruits
Carrots
Spinach

SILICON

Asparagus
Spinach
Lettuce
Barley
Figs
Berries
Oatmeal
Bran
Grapes
Strawberries
Cherries
Apples
Celery
Beets
Parsnips
Black Figs

Radishes
Chard
Onions
Eggs
Oranges

SODIUM

Wheat Bread
Rye Bread
Buttermilk
Cream Cheese
Codfish
Halibut
Mackerel
Salmon
Bananas
Celery
Dandelions
Lettuce
Spinach
Sweet Potato
Milk
American Cheese
Beet
Watercress

SULPHUR

Watercress
Asparagus
Cabbage
Garlic
Grapes
Onions
Beans
Bran
Bread
Brussels Sprouts
Cauliflower
Cheese

Clams	Oysters
Eggs	Peas
Nuts	Chard
Fish	Wheat
Oats	

FATS AND OILS

Fats and oils are very important in a diet. One of their best sources in a vegetarian diet is nuts. The fat content of nuts is very high, sometimes well over 50%.

All fats are made up of three elements—carbon, hydrogen, and oxygen. These elements are the most concentrated forms of fuel for our bodies to burn. They give twice as much heat as either proteins or carbohydrates. During digestion fats are absorbed partly into the small intestine and partly into the lymph. They ultimately go into the bloodstream.

Storage of fats takes place in depositories under the skin in the tissues of most organs, in the mesentery (the membranes of the peritoneum), and around the kidneys. When these fat storage deposits are filled, new fats pass into the liver.

You may cut down your intake of fats, but remember: you have a definite need for fat in your diet. In the form of phospholipids, fats play an important role in nourishing the brain. Fats are essential in forming acetate, a crucial element in the energy-producing cycles of your body. Sterols, essential to life, are a class of compounds derived from fats.

The fats and oils from nuts do not contain, as far as we can tell, any Vitamin D. But margarines made from nut oils can be fortified with this important vitamin, so that they are as beneficial in this respect as butter.

Though it was once thought nut butters and oils contained no vitamin A, modern researchers have found some nut oils in fact contain substantial quantities.

Since nuts contain a considerable amount of basic amino acids, butter made from nuts has a high biological value. When eaten by nursing and pregnant mothers, nut oils also improve the quality of their milk.

The digestibility of nuts increases as much as 10 percent when they are turned into butter, since the digestive juices of our bodies can only work imperfectly on nuts not ground by the teeth and broken down (they are passed undigested into the alimentary canal). Unfortunately, most commercial butters are made from roasted nuts which have been heavily salted. The heat involved during this process develops free fatty acids and destroys the B-complex vitamins. Salt and nuts interfere with their digestibility.

As one of the most concentrated foods, nuts have as high a nutritional value as any animal product (almonds and cashews taken together) except cheese. The fat in all nut butters is more easily digested than dairy butter and, unlike animal fats, mixes with water and forms an easily digested emulsion.

The digestion of fats requires the presence of organic sodium in your food. Sodium is principally an alkaline element in the process of saponification, which takes place when the pancreatic juice, bile, and intestinal juices come into contact with fats. If you eat fresh vegetables and fruits with nuts, the organic sodium found in these foods will accomplish saponification.

Much of a nut's vitamins are found in its skin, so leave this on when eating them. When nuts are salted and roasted, these vitamins are destroyed.

In conclusion, a vegetarian diet need not be low in protein. If the rules relating to protein intake, digestion, and assimilation are followed, the vegetarian should have no worry about an adequate diet.

Now we look at the combinations in which foods can be eaten to assure the body of their maximum benefit.

FOOD VALUES

Where no vitamin values are given in this table it is because they have not yet been determined. In any case, the amount present probably is insignificant for ordinary nutritional purposes, except in the case of vitamin B2.

UNIT EQUIVALENTS:

Vitamin A

1 International unit = 2 Sherman Units

= 0.6 microgram (gamma, y) of B carotene

Vitamin B1 (Thiamine Chloride)

1 International unit = 3 micrograms (gamma, y)

= 0.003 milligram

= 2 Sherman units

Vitamin C (Ascorbic Acid, Cevitamin Acid)

1 milligram = 20 International units

= 2 Sherman units

Vitamin B2 (Riboflavin)

1 milligram = 333 Sherman-Bourquin units

= 1000 micrograms (gamma, y)

	MEASURE Ordinary	Ounces	Vitamin A I.U	Vitamin B1 I.U	Vitamin C Mill.	Vitamin B2 Mill.
BREADS & CEREALS						
Barley, whole grain	1 tblsp.	½	0	3.3	—	0.001
" , pearled	1 tblsp.	½	0	0	—	
Biscuits, baking powder	1 biscuit		19	3	—	
Bread, Boston brown	1 slice 3″ diam. ⅜″ thick	¾	55	13	—	
" , white, made with milk	1 slice 3″x3½″x½″	¾	10	3.8	—	0.0121
" , white, made with water	1 slice 3″x3½″x½″	¾	10	3.7	—	0.006
" , 100% wheat	1 slice 3″x3″x⅜″	1	70	27	—	
" , rye	1 slice 3″x3″x⅜″	1		14	—	
Corn, whole grain yellow	1 cup	5	1,200	72	11	0.05
" , flakes, cereal	1 cup	1½		trace	0	
" , meal, white	1 cup	5	0	143		
" , meal, yellow	1 cup	5	1,200	110		
Crackers, Graham	1 cracker		26	8	0	
Custard, baked	¾ cup	3	650	21	1	

				30–70		
Flour, rye	1 cup	5	500	180	0	
" , 100% whole, unbleached	1 cup	4	150	33	0	
" , white, bleached	1 cup	4	130	19	0	
" , white, pastry	1 cup	4	130	49	0	
" , white, plus germ	1 cup	4			0	
Griddlecakes	1 medium	2	200	11	0.5	
Muffins, plain w. egg	1 muffin		135	9	0	
" , plain, without egg	1 muffin		48	8	0	
" , bran, with egg	1 muffin		260	50	0	
" , bran, without egg	1 muffin		170	52	0	
Oatmeal, whole grain	½ cup	1¾	0	165	0	0.02
" , quick cooking	½ cup	1¾	0	130	0	0.022
Oats, rolled, packaged	½ cup	1¾	0	121	0	
" , rolled, cooked	½ cup	1¾	0	121	0	
Rice, brown	2 tblsp.	1	17	15	0	
" , polished	2 tblsp.	1	0	0	0	
Rolls	1 roll	1½	74	9	0	
Rye, whole grain	1 cup	5	0	210	0	0.02
Wheat, whole grain	1 tblsp.	½	50	23	4	
" , whole grain, cooked	1 tblsp.	½	50	23	0	
" , bran	1 tblsp.	½	85	28	0	
" , farina, light	1 tblsp.	½	0	0.2	0	0
" , germ	1 tblsp.	½	90	80	0	0.10

BREAD & CEREALS	Ordinary MEASURE	Ounces	Vitamin A I.U	Vitamin BI I.U	Vitamin C Mill.	Vitamin B2 Mill.
Wheat, puffed	½ cup	½	30	0	0	0.001
" , semolina	1 tblsp.	½		7		
" , shredded	1 biscuit	1	4	20		0.10
Wheat, stone-ground	1 tblsp.	½	40	22	3	0.015
DAIRY PRODUCTS						
Butter	1 square	½	315	0	trace	
Buttermilk	1 large glass	8	0	35	2	0.310
Cheese, Am. Cheddar	1" cube	¾	420	3	0	0.12
" , Camembert	1" cube	¾	750		0	
" , cottage, skim	1 tblsp.	¾	70	0.6	0	0.068
" , creamed, soft	1 tblsp.	½	310		0	0.017
" , creamed, full	piece 2"x1"	1	500		0	0.02
" , Edam	1" cube	¾	300		0	
" , pimento (kraft)	1" cube	¾	500		0	
" , Roquefort	1" cube	¾	850		0	
" , Swiss (kraft)	piece 4"x4"	¾	440		0	
Cream, 20% fat	1 tblsp.	3/5	64	2	trace	
Cream, 40% fat	1 tblsp.	3/5	132	1.6	trace	
Eggs, whole	1 egg	1½	900	19	0	0.25
" , white	1 white	9/10	0	trace	0	0.14

" , yolk	1 yolk	6/10	900	19	0	0.11
" , soft-boiled	1 egg	6/10	900	19	0	
" , hard-boiled	1 egg	6/10	900	19	0	
Milk, whole, fresh, raw	1 quart	32	1,400	150	19	1.20
Milk, whole, fresh, raw	1 glass	6	260	28	3.5	0.23
" , whole, fresh, pasteur.	1 glass	6	260	22	3.0	0.23
" , dried, reconstituted	1 glass	6	260	20	2.0	0.20
" , evaporated	1 tumbler	4	190	15	3.5	0.35
" , condensed, sweetened	½ cup	¾	45	10		
" , skim, fresh	1 tblsp.		trace	25	4.0	0.17
" , skim, dried powder	1 glass	6	0	8	0.7	0.09
" , shake, ice cream	1 tblsp.	12	0	37	4	

MEAT & FISH

Bacon, fried	5 slices	½		5	0	0.06
Beef, lean, top round	¼ lb.	4	40	45	2.2	0.029
Chicken, light meat	¼ lb.	4		30	0	0.078
Chicken, dark meat	¼ lb.	4		42	0	2.0
Chicken liver	⅛ lb.	2	17,000	50	11	0.11
Cod, steak, fresh	¼ lb.	4	2	34	0	0.40
Crab	¼ lb.	4	2,200	45	5	0.21
Halibut, muscle	¼ lb.	4		32		
Ham, smoked, lean	¼ lb.	4		540		

MEAT & FISH

	Ordinary	MEASURE Ounces	Vitamin A I.U	Vitamin B1 I.U	Vitamin C Mill.	Vitamin B2 Mill.
Herring, whole	¼ lb.	4	1,700	20		0.12
Kidney, beef or calf	¼ lb.	4	450	105	12	1.6
Lamb, chop, lean	¼ lb.	4	trace	90	2	
Liver, beef, fresh	¼ lb.	4	46,000	100	34	3.4
Mackerel	¼ lb.	4		34		
Mutton, lean	¼ lb.	4		68		
Oysters, raw	⅓ cup	3½	420	75	3	0.46
Pork chop, lean	¼ lb.	4	0	515	2	
Pork, loin, lean	¼ lb.	4	0	515	2	0.28
Prawns, boiled	¼ lb.	4	1,100	20	0	0.11
Salmon, fresh, canned	¼ lb.	4	340	trace		0.27
Sardines, canned in oil	⅛ lb.	2	200	17		
Sweetbreads, fresh	¼ lb.	4		120		
Tongue, beef or sheep	¼ lb.	4		35		
Trout, fresh-water	¼ lb.	4		33		
Veal, muscle, cooked	¼ lb.	4	40	45	2	0.17
Whiting, Atlantic	¼ lb.	4	400	45		

FRUITS

Apples, raw, average	1 medium	6	50	8	10	0.06
" , applesauce	½ cup	4½			9	
" , Juice	1 tumbler	6			5	
Apricots, fresh	1 medium	1⅓	1,000	3.5	2	0.04
" , dried	4 halves	⅗	540	8	0	0.009
" , dried, sulphured	4 halves	⅗	540	3	2	0.005
Avocado, California	½ avocado	4	64	40	25	0.19
Bananas	1 medium	5½	230	28	7	0.07
Blackberries	1 cup	5¾	230	10	15	
Blueberries	1 cup	5¼	150	21	8	0.021
Cantaloupe	½ mellon	13½	770	73	60	0.25
Cherries, fresh, bing	10 cherries	2⅓	75	12	13	
Cranberries, fresh	1 cup	3¾	20	0	20	0
Cranberries, Juice	½ cup	2			7	0
Currant, black fresh	1 cup	3¾		11	220	
Currant, red, fresh	1 cup	3¾		16	55	
Dates, fresh	4 dates	1½	35	12	0	0.012
Dates, dried	4 dates	1½	15	8.5	0	0
Figs, fresh	3 small	4	90	30	2.3	0.06
Figs, dried	3 small	2⅕	32	30	0	
Gooseberries, canned	1 cup	4	330	56	34	
Grapes, white, seedless	½ bunch	4	22	11	2.2	0

	MEASURE Ordinary	Ounces	Vitamin A I.U	Vitamin B1 I.U	Vitamin C Mill.	Vitamin B2 Mill.
Guava	1 guava	¾	22	2	30	0.006
Lemon	1 large	3⅗	0		55	
Lemon, Juice	2 tblsp.	1	0		15	0.001
Lime juice, fresh	2 tblsp.	1	8		10	
Mangoes	1 mango	3	850	17	25	0.05
Olives, green	6 olives	2	85	trace	0	
Olives, mission	6 olives	2	28	trace	0	
Orange, pulp	1 large	9½	80–270	95	80	0.24
Orange, Juice, fresh	1 tumbler	6	540	59	98	0.012
Orange, Juice Canned	1 tumbler	6	540	59	72	
Papayas	1 papaya	3	1,800	7	46	0.015
Peaches, fresh	1 medium	4	900	28	3.4	0.008
Peaches, canned	2 halves	3	900	22	1.7	
Pears, fresh, Bartlett	1 pear	3⅕	6	5	3	0.015
Pineapple, fresh	1 slice ⅜″	1⅜	90	13	2.6	0.006
Pineapple, Canned	1 slice ⅜″	1⅜	90	7	2.3	
Pineapple, Juice, canned	1 tumbler	6	90	35	12	
Plums, fresh	2 plums	3⅘	210	17	5.5	0.027
Plums, canned	2 plums	3⅘	200	15	5	
Pomegranate	1 pomegranate	6	0		20	
Prunes	4 prunes	1⅖	350	24	trace	0.3

Quince	1 quince	4		11		
Raisins	¼ cup	1	28	21	0	0.04
Raspberries	1 cup	4⅗	270	trace	33	
Strawberries	½ box	6	340	trace	93	
Tangerines	1 tangerine	2	280	22	28	0.022
Watermelon	1 slice 6″¾	11	0	25	15	0.18

VEGETABLES

Artichokes	1 artichoke	8½	250	70	15	0.025
Asparagus, green	2 stalks	1⅓	130	22	19	
Beans, baked	1 cup	4	15	150	0	
" , kidney, fresh	½ cup	3	27	63	0	0.025
" , navy, dried	½ cup	3½	27	128	0	
" , lima, fresh	½ cup	3	0	100	13	0.25
" , string or snap	½ cup	3½	600	25	8	0.08
" , string, canned	½ cup	3½	600	11	2	
" , runner, green	½ cup	3½	700	40	5	
" , soy black	½ cup	3½	900	100	46	
" , soy, white	½ cup	3½	140	250		
" , wax, butter, yellow	½ cup	3½	410	30	16	
Beets, Root	½ cup diced	5	70	24	5	

VEGETABLES	MEASURE Ordinary	Ounces	Vitamin A I.U	Vitamin B1 I.U	Vitamin C Mill.	Vitamin B2 Mill.
Broccoli, fresh	1 cup	4	4,000	38	80	
Brussels sprouts	6 sprouts	4	1,100	65	100	
Cabbage, white, raw	1 cup	3⅓	800	25	25	0.04
Cabbage, white, cooked	1 cup	3½	50	20	12	
Carrots, raw	1 cup diced	4¾	2,700	32	8	0.03
Carrots, cooked	1 cup diced	4¾	2,700	32	5	
Carrots, canned, strained	1 cup diced	4¾	2,700	13	3	
Cauliflower, raw	¼ head	3	49	46	33	0.065
Cauliflower, cooked	¼ head	3		35	33	
Celery, green stems	2 stalks 7″	1½	320		2	
Celery, blanched stems	2 stalks 7″	1½	2	5	2	
Chard (beet tops) raw	½ cup	5⅕	12,000	20	43	
Chard beet cooked	½ cup	5⅕	12,000	15	28	
Chicory (escarole) raw	4 leaves	3½	9,500		5	0.022
Chives	1 teasp.	⅕			2	
Collards, fresh raw	½ cup	3⅗	2,200	68	50	0.3
Collards, cooked	½ cup	3⅗	2,200	50	22	
Corn, yellow, whole	¼ cup	1⅘	250	25	5	0.018
Corn, sweet, canned	½ cup	3½	120	30	11	
Cucumbers, raw	½ of 10″	6½	0–20	55	18	0.003
Dandelion greens	1 cup	3½	12,500			

Eggplant	3 slices 4"	6⅓	70	43	8	0.10
Endive	3 stalks 6"	7⅓	4,200	70	20	
Garlic	1 clove	¼	0		2	0.50
Kale, raw	1 cup	3⅖	9,000	59	140	
Kale, cooked	1 cup	3⅖	9,000	45	28	
Kohlrabi	1 cup ½"	5			39	
Leek	1 leek 7"	1	17	8	7	
Lentils	2 tblsp.	1	25	14		0.022
Lettuce, Romaine	2 leaves 9"	¾	1,300	4	1	0.03
Lettuce, Iceberg, head	¼ L. Head	2½	150	20	4.5	0.05
Mustard greens	½ cup	2⅓	100	30		
Okra	5 pods	2	85	23	6	0.26
Onions, fresh	1 medium	2	6,200			
Onions, fresh, stewed	1 medium	2	0	10		
Parsley	4 stems	½	1,000		11	
Parsnips	17"x2"	6¾	380	66	38	
Peas, fresh	½ cup	2½	530	85	20	0.026
Peppers, green	1 pepper	2½	600	69	0.12	
Peppers, red	1 pepper	2½	2,200		135	
Potatoes, yellow, sweet	½ medium	3⅗	8,000	31	20	0.02
Potatoes, yellow, sweet, cooked	½ medium	3⅗	4,000	25	10	
Potatoes, white	1 medium	5⅓	60	93	30	
Potatoes, white cooked	1 medium	5⅓	40	74	30	

	Ordinary MEASURE	Ounces	Vitamin A I.U	Vitamin B1 I.U	Vitamin C Mill.	Vitamin B2 Mill.
Rutabagas	1 cup	5	10	28	22	0.13
Sauerkraut, fresh	1 cup	5		trace	16	
Sauerkraut, cooked	1 cup	5			3	
Sauerkraut, juice	2 tblsp.	1			4	
Spinach, raw	½ cup chop	3⅗	14,000	37	53	0.065
Spinach, cooked	½ cup chop	3⅗	14,000	30	26	
Squash, winter, Hubbard	½ cup	4	2,900	21	3.5	
Squash, summer, winter	½ cup	4	170	16	3.5	
Tapioca	2 tblsp.	1	0	0	0	0
Tomatoes	1 medium	7	6,000	52	50	0.10
Tomatoes, canned	½ cup	4¼	3,600	25	24	
Tomatoes, juice, canned	½ cup	6	5,300	25	25	0.25
Turnip greens	1 tumbler	3	6,000	38	42	
Turnip, cooked	½ cup	3	6,000	25	10	
Watercress	½ bunch	1½	2,000	28	22	
NUTS						
Almonds	10 nuts	⅗	0	7	0.5	0.028
Cashews	5 nuts	½	19	12	5	
Chestnuts	2 nuts	½	0	1	0.5	0.014
Cocoanut, shredded	1 tblsp.	⅓	0	1	0.5	
Cocoanut, milk, fresh	1 cup	8	0	0	4	

Hazel	10 nuts	½		28	2	
Peanuts, whole, Spanish	⅓ cup	1½	17	146	4	0.3
Peanuts, shelled	⅓ cup	1½	17	146	4	0.3
Peanuts, roasted	⅓ cup	1½	17	33	4	
Peanut butter	2 tblsp.	1½	17	125	0	
Pecans	12 nuts	½	14			
Pistachio	15 nuts	½	14			
Walnuts	12 nuts	½	190	16	3.5	

MISCELLANEOUS

Corn oil	1 tblsp.		0	0	0	0
Cottonseed oil			0	0	0	0
Ice cream, made with skim milk	8		0	15	3	
Lard			0	0	0	0
Mayonnaise	1 tblsp.		30	0.5	0	
Pie, apple	1 serving		90	14	0	
Pie, blueberry	1 serving		62	9	3	
Pie, chocolate	1 serving		440	10	0	
Soup, black bean	1 cup		70	11	0.5	
Soup, split pea	1 cup		145	18	0	

MISCELLANEOUS

	MEASURE		Vitamin A I.U	Vitamin B1 I.U	Vitamin C Mill.	Vitamin B2 Mill.
	Ordinary	Ounces				
Soup, tomato	1 cup	4	1,480	10	9	
Soup, vegetable	1 cup	4	276	9	4	
Sugar			0	0	0	0
Tea			0	0	0	0
Coffee			0	0	0	0
Cocoa	2 tblsp.	½	0	4	0	0
Beer	1 glass	6	0	4	0	0
Yeast, baker's compress	1 cake	2	0	100	1	1.4
Yeast, baker's dried	1 cake	½	0	70		0.5
Yeast, brewer's, fresh	1 cake	2	100	220		0.85
Yeast, brewer's, dried	1 cake	½		8–500		0.4

CHAPTER FOUR

UNDERSTANDING FOOD COMBINING

The following menus and much of the research material were compiled from years of extensive work by one of the world's most renowned nutritionists, Dr. Herbert M. Shelton, at his health school in San Antonio, Texas. We also recommend that you read his book, *Food Combining Made Easy*.

The area of food combining in nutrition is a relatively new one. The information in this chapter is meant as a guide to digestion, not as a list of hard and fast rules to be applied apart from other nutritional information found elsewhere in this book.

Let us review the classifications of foods here because they are essential to a full understanding of what follows.

A common misconception concerning nutrition is that the most important part of any meal is planning it so that it is balanced and full of life sustaining nutrients. This is important but you must go one step further: combine your foods to gain the best digestion, assimilation and utilization.

Foods eaten raw or cooked can not be used directly by the body; They must first be broken down into proteins, fats and carbohydrates. The digestive process is very complex and deals with the functions of disintegration, refinement, and standardization of sugars, mineral salts, proteins, carbohydrates, vitamins, and fats. The emphasis in this chapter will be on the digestion of foods in the mouth and stomach.

It is important to know exactly what type of nutritional value the food you consume contains. The following classifications will assist you in understanding food combining:

PROTEINS:

Nuts	All Cereals	Dry Beans
Dry Peas	Soy Beans	Peanuts
Avocados	Cheese	Olives
Fowl	Milk	Coconut
Lean Meat	Fish	

CARBOHYDRATES: Starches and Sugars:

Starches:

Dry Peas	Hubbard Squash	Jerusalem Artichokes
All Cereals	Potatoes	Banana Squash
Peanuts	Caladium Root	Flour
Pumpkin	Cakes	Pastas
Bread	Pies	
Dry Beans	Chestnuts	

Mildly Starchy:

Cauliflower	Beets	Carrots
Rutabaga	Salsify	

Syrups and Sugars:

Brown Sugar	Cane Syrup	Molasses
Maple Syrup	Milk Sugar	
White Sugar	Honey	

Sweet Fruits:

Bananas	Dates	Figs
Raisins	Grapes	Prunes
Sun-dried Pears	Persimmons	

FATS:

Olive Oil	Soy Oil	Lard
Sesame Oil	Corn Oil	Butter
Cream	Nut Oils	Butter Substitutes
Pecans	Avocados	Most Nuts
Fat Meats	Sunflower Seed Oil	Cotton Seed Oil

ACID FRUITS:

Oranges	Grapefruit	Pineapples
Pomegranates	Sour Apples	Limes
Sour Peaches	Tomatoes	Sour Grapes
Lemons	Sour Plums	Sour Cherries

Sub-Acid Fruits:

Fresh Figs	Pineapples	Sweet Cherries
Papayas	Pears	Sweet Apples
Apricots	Sweet Peaches	Huckleberries
Mangoes	Sweet Plums	

NON-STARCHY AND GREEN VEGETABLES:

Lettuce	Cabbage	Green Peas
Chicory	Brussels Sprouts	Endive
Broccoli	Dandelion	Cauliflower
Spinach	Chard	Collards
Turnip Tops	Chinese Cabbage	Beet Tops
Cow-slip	Mustard	Okra
Turnips	Kale	Chive
Green Beans	Green Corn	Dock (buckwheat)
Sorrel	Cucumber	Eggplant
Watercress	Parsley	Kohlrabi
Leeks	Garlic	Scallions
Escarole	Onions	Rhubarb
Summer Squash	Cardoon	Zucchini
Sweet Pepper	Asparagus	Bamboo Sprouts
Celery	Broccoli	Radishes

MELONS:

Watermelon	Muskmelon	Honeydew
Cantaloupe	Banana Melon	Pie Melon
Wintermelon	Casaba	Crenshaw Melon
	Persian Melon	Nutmeg Melon

Once you classify foods you eat, it will be easier to understand how the digestive system works. Digestion is slightly different for each food and this can make an important difference in how well you benefit from the food you eat.

DIGESTION

Since your body cannot directly use foods in the form in which you eat them, your system must break foods down through a series of changes before using them. This breaking-down process of digestion is done by a group of substances known as enzymes.

Understanding how an enzyme works is important to understanding digestion. Enzymes are catalysts. They have the ability to cause un-related substances to combine when brought into contact with the third substance (enzyme catalyst). The enzyme's function is to act as this third or binding substance. The unique part of the enzyme's work is that it causes two or more substances to combine without entering into the combination or sharing in the reaction.

Both plants and animals manufacture soluble enzymes which are colloidal in nature but resistant to heat. Enzymes can cause complex food particles to be broken down into simpler compounds which the body can more easily assimilate and utilize. Enzymes are also unique in that they react only on one type of food substance which makes their action very specific.

Another characteristic of an enzyme is that it is specific in its action. It acts only upon one class of food substances. This means the enzymes which act upon carbohydrates such as potatoes and dry beans cannot act upon proteins, fats, or salts. There are specific groups of enzymes in your body to act upon every type of food.

This point becomes even more important when you realize there are many stages of digestion for each type of food and every stage requires the action of a different enzyme. These enzyme actions are progressive; if a food being digested reaches the third enzyme, the first two enzymes must have done their work for the third to act effectively.

In protein digestion a substance called *pepsin* first converts the protein into *peptones*, which in turn are converted to amino acids by another enzyme. If the pepsin hasn't done its work of converting the protein into peptones, the next enzyme will be unable to convert it into amino acids.

The substance upon which an enzyme acts is called a substrate. Thus starch is a substrate of ptyalin. Each enzyme is apparently adapted to a certain definite structure, the structure of its substrate.

Let's look now at what type of action takes place at each step of digestion. Digestion begins in the mouth, where all foods are broken up by action of chewing and saturation with saliva. Digestion stops for all foods in the mouth except starch. There is an enzyme in saliva called *ptyalin*, whose substrate is starch. While the starch is still in the mouth, ptyalin breaks it down into a complex sugar called maltose. Now all food is swallowed to continue digestion. Maltose is further acted upon in the intestine by the enzyme maltase, which converts it into a simple sugar called dextrose.

Another enzyme involved in starch digestion is *amylase*. Amylase, an enzyme of the pancreatic system, acts upon starch much in the same way as ptyalin. In this way, starch that escapes digestion in the mouth and stomach may be split into maltose and achroo-dextrane. Otherwise, the maltase would be unable to act upon it.

The environment in which an enzyme works is also important. Ptyalin, for example, is destroyed by either a mild acid environment or a strong alkaline medium. To operate properly, ptyalin needs a mild alkaline medium. It is this limitation of the enzyme that makes important the manner in which you mix your starches. If starches are mixed with a food high in acid, or with a food that stimulates acid secretion in the stomach, the work of ptyalin is brought to a stop.

Your stomach (gastric) juices range from nearly neutral to strongly acid, depending on the character of the food you have eaten. Gastric juices contain three enzymes—pepsin, lipase, and rennin. Pepsin acts only on proteins and only in an acid environment, for it is destroyed by an alkali. Low temperature (drinking an ice cold liquid) suspends its action, while alcohol speeds it up. The other two gastric enzymes, lipase and rennin, have different functions. Lipase has a slight action on fats. Rennin coagulates milk.

The secretions of your body are adapted to the different foods consumed. The elements and their proportions which compose the gastric juices at any given moment are dependent on food present at that moment.

Even the flow of saliva is governed by the nature of the foodstuffs present. Saliva flows freely in response to weak acids but may not flow at all in the presence of a weak alkali. The body can protect itself from a noxious substance by producing a heavy flow of saliva which will flush away the disagreeable material.

The important point to keep in mind is this: the kind of juice produced in the body during digestion is determined by the purpose it must serve.

COMBINATIONS—GOOD AND BAD

Since different enzymes work on different foods and these enzymes differ in the environment they need to work well, you can see how important it is to know what combinations of food are compatible. Let's now take a closer look at the possible combinations of foods and relate them to the facts of digestion.

Acid—Starch

When a weak acid is introduced into the mouth, the ptyalin in the saliva is destroyed. When this happens, the digestion of starch must come to a halt. Yet many people eat acid fruit before their breakfast cereal without noticing any ill effects. The reason for this is that any starch that escapes the action of ptyalin will be acted upon later by the pancreatic juices. The final result may be satisfactory. It is reasonable to assume, however, that the greater the work done by the saliva, the lighter the work load on the other secretions and the better the chances digestion will be more complete.

It appears, then, that an acid-starch combination cuts down the efficiency of starch digestion. Foods that suspend salivary digestion or destroy ptyalin include: vinegar, tomatoes, berries, oranges, lemons, limes, grapefruit, sour apples, grapes, pineapples, and other sour fruit. To obtain the most efficient digestion of your foods, you might do well to eat acid foods and starches separately.

Protein—Starch

When you eat carbohydrates the stomach produces a gastric juice to digest carbohydrates. This juice has a distinctly different composition from that which the stomach secretes when proteins are present. To digest proteins your system requires an acid medium. This digestion stops when a distinctly alkaline mixture is made. The acid favorable to digestion of proteins inhibits digestion of starches. Conversely, starch digestion inhibits protein digestion.

When you eat a piece of bread, the first thing that happens in the stomach is the secretion of an almost neutral juice in response to the starch that must be digested. Once this starch is digested, a second substance is poured into the stomach to digest the protein of the bread. The starch and protein from the same piece of bread are not digested simultaneously. Instead, the secretions are adjusted efficiently in both character and timing to the changing needs of the complex food substance present.

The concepts outlined in this chapter may seem to be contradictory on one point. That is, "How can we separate our protein and starches when Nature combines different foods?" On the surface it may seem to be a contradiction. However, the difference between digestion of a single food, regardless of its complexity and various nutrients, and the digestion of a mixture of different foods is considerable. To cite an example, a potato contains an incomplete protein and is mostly starch. However, the body has no trouble in pouring out different digestive juices to digest the protein and starch. But your digestive system is not fully able to adjust so easily when two foods are eaten which necessitate different digestive mediums.

A simple everyday act of putting a piece of meat (protein) between two pieces of bread (starch) to make a sandwich can complicate the digestion of these foods tremendously. Instead of an almost neutral gastric juice being poured into the stomach during the first two hours of digestion, as happened with the single piece of bread, a highly acid juice is secreted immediately. You already know that a highly acid medium inhibits or completely halts starch digestion. In the ingestion of your meat sandwich the digestion of the starch comes almost to an end.

It is clear that starch and protein require opposite media to be digested. The starch needs an alkaline medium and the protein needs an acid medium. The two cannot easily exist together.

One of the ways to avoid such digestive interference of one type of food with another is to eat the protein part of a meal first. Then it can digest in the lower end of the stomach. By eating the starch part of the meal last, you allow it to be digested in the mouth and the upper end of the stomach.

When you eat starch and protein together, as in a cheese or meat sandwich, the stomach has no mechanism to separate the two intermixed substances; therefore the digestion of one or both might be incomplete. By separating your protein foods from carbohydrate foods, you facilitate the digestion of both. The simple rule to follow is this: cereals, bread, potatoes, and other starch foods should be eaten separately from eggs, cheese, fish, and other protein foods.

Protein—Protein

The combination of proteins with other proteins might at first seem like a good one. It would be a good combination if all proteins had the same character and the same composition and were all associated with the same food factors. But they do not and are not. Even among proteins the character, composition, and association with other food factors are not the same, and these distinctions require modifications of digestive juices and different timings of the secretions which must be poured out for the most efficient digestion of these foods.

For instance, milk, meat and eggs receive their strongest secretion for digestion at different times. The strongest juice is poured out on meat in the first hour of digestion, on milk in the last hour. Eggs receive their strongest juice secretion at a time in between the first and last hours. It might be advisable then to avoid eating eggs at the same time as either flesh or milk.

Since the digestive processes change to meet the requirements of each protein food, it is hard for your system to adjust to meet the digestive needs of two different proteins eaten together. As a general rule it is all right to eat two kinds of the same protein food at the same time. Two kinds of flesh together, or two different nuts should not cause any problem in digestion, since they are digested in approximately the same patterns. It is when flesh and nuts are eaten together that your system might run into trouble digesting the various kinds of proteins effectively. By taking one protein food at a meal, you can assure greater efficiency in digestion. The rule then is to eat only one concentrated protein food at a meal.

While the objection might be raised that you need more than one kind of protein because protein foods vary so much in their amino acid content, this is only a problem on the surface. For you do eat more than one meal a day and can spread your proteins over several meals rather than eat them all at one meal.

In a diet de-emphasizing meat proteins and relying on plant sources for this vital substance, the combinations concerning you most are nuts and eggs, nuts and milk, nuts and cheese, etc.

Acid—Protein

The enzyme pepsin is responsible for splitting up complex protein substances during digestion. Since pepsin acts only in an acid medium, the presence of alkaline will bring pepsin's work to a halt. When you eat protein, the gastric juice secreted in the stomach is acid, offering a favorable environment for the action of pepsin to take place and facilitating the digestion of proteins.

It would be a mistake to assume, however, that eating acids with proteins would assist in the digestion of these proteins. The presence of acids inhibits the outpouring of gastric juices, interfering with the digestion of proteins.

Protein digestion is affected by any strong acid, such as that of an orange, lemon or other acidic fruit. The strong acid destroys the pepsin enzyme which is needed to convert the protein into amino acids. The basic fact to remember is: when acid is present in the mouth and stomach, gastric juices are not secreted. This leaves the bulk in the stomach to putrify or ferment. In the warm, moist intestine meat rots quickly.

Under normal conditions your stomach will secrete all the acid you need for the pepsin enzyme to digest a reasonable quantity of protein, and the presence of acid in the mouth and stomach changes these conditions. Therefore it is suggested that you avoid eating proteins and acids at the same meals.

There is an exception to this rule—nuts and cheese can be eaten with acid fruits. While this is not an ideal combination, the nuts and cheese do contain considerable oil and fat which will not decompose as quickly as other protein foods when they are not immediately digested. Furthermore, acids do not delay the digestion of nuts and cheeses as they do the digestion of other protein foods, because nuts and cheese contain enough fat to inhibit gastric secretion for a longer time than do the presence of acids.

In looking at the combination of proteins and acids, you can once more see that a de-emphasis on meats in your diet and their replacement with plant sources of protein can play a role in helping you efficiently use the food you eat. Nuts and cheese are both good sources of protein and will not give you the trouble of other protein foods when combined with acids.

Fat–Protein

Foods which contain a high percentage of fat can influence your appetite by reducing the amount of secretions which affect your desire for food. Hydrochloric acid and pepsin are also affected by the amount of fat in the stomach and can lower the amounts of the two protein-splitting enzymes by half.

Foods that contain fat within themselves, like nuts and cheese, require a longer time to be digested than protein foods without fats. Eggs and cheese should not be consumed with milk or foods containing oils.

It is well-known that green vegetables, especially uncooked ones, counteract the inhibiting effect of fat. If you must have fat with your protein, you may offset its inhibiting effect by also eating green substances. Even so, the general suggestion is to eat fats and proteins at separate times.

Sugar–Protein

Sugars can have the same nullifying effect on the digestion of proteins as when an acidic fruit and protein are combined together. Sugars tend to inhibit the secretion of gastric juice and disrupt the natural motility of the stomach.

Sugars should be eaten alone. Sugar will digest very quickly if you have not eaten protein or carbohydrates at the same meal. Sugars digest in the intestine and will ferment causing gas and indigestion if held up for more than an hour in the stomach. Sugars (desserts) should be eaten before the main course allowing for quicker and more complete digestion.

The digestion of starch occurs in the mouth and small intestine. Starch is much more quickly assimilated than protein. Starches stay in the stomach for a short time, just long enough to be emulsified into a semi-liquid form.

Sugar—Starch

Starch digestion begins normally in the mouth and continues for some time in the stomach. Sugars, however, are not digested until they reach the small intestine. When eaten alone, sugar is quickly sent out of the stomach into the intestine, but if sugar is eaten with another food type that causes it to be held up in the stomach it will ferment very quickly in the warmth and moisture. Eating a combination of starch and sugar almost guarantees acid fermentation.

Combining sugar and starch is a very common mistake. Many people combine jams, honey, molasses, syrups, etc. with cakes, breads, pastries, and cereals. Sugar on cereal is another common mixture. The result of such combinations may be a sour stomach, sour eructations, and other evidence of indigestion. A better understanding of how starches and sugars are digested can help you overcome these consequences.

The same uncomfortable results can come from mixing sweet fruits with starches. Breads containing dates, raisins, figs, etc., should be avoided. Even honey or syrup with hot cakes can cause fermentation of the sugar in the stomach.

The presence of sugar with starch also interferes with the digestion of the starch. When sugar is taken into the mouth, there is an outpouring of saliva, but it does not contain the ptyalin needed to start starch digestion.

Therefore some mixtures can cause unpleasant digestion or indigestion. Bread and butter, for example, cause no problems, but if sugar or jam or marmalade are added trouble is likely to follow. In every case combining starch with sugar invites sugar fermentation in the stomach. It is advisable then to eat your starch and your sugars at different times.

EAT SMALL MEALS

It is becoming increasingly known that you can digest your food best if you don't fill your stomach with large amounts of food at one time. With an understanding of food combining and the other information covered in this book, you might do well to eat several small meals a day, rather than the usual three big ones. Not only will this facilitate digestion, it will make it easier to avoid ineffective combinations of foods. In this way you can expect to take fuller advantage of the food you eat by following the guidelines you've learned about how your digestive system operates.

CHAPTER FIVE

RATIONAL FASTING

The practice of fasting has long been associated with a vegetarian diet. It has also been accepted throughout most of history as a form of therapy. But you will not find any wild claims of cures from fasting in this chapter, for that is not our purpose. What you will find is some solid information that we hope will be useful if you think of going on a fast for whatever reason. It is unfortunate, but true, that most people who undertake a fast know little or nothing about it. This, of course, can be dangerous. These people often cause themselves unnecessary side effects. We intend in this chapter to give you all the essential facts you might need to know about fasting.

There are many fasts—fruit fasts, vegetable fasts, and the most common form, total abstinence from all foods but not from water. It is this last fast we are most concerned with here: the elimination of all foods for some length of time.

We will not claim that fasting is a cure for any disease or ailment. Healing or repair of any cell is an internal process. To speed the healing process the system should not be overburdened with trying to clean the putrefied matter which accumulates in the intestinal tract. Fasting allows much of this matter to be eliminated and thus facilitates the rejuvenating functions.

If you are making a change in your diet, for instance switching from a meat protein oriented diet to a vegetable-plant-protein oriented diet, it might help your system adjust to the change if you fast for a while between the times you stop eating meat and begin your full vegetarian diet. By doing this you will allow your body to flush out many of the toxins accumulated from the meat you have been eating. Many chemicals which enter our bodies in our food supply, the air we breathe and the water we drink. Nearly one hundred different pollutants are consumed in an average day. Many of these toxic substances can't be metabolized and are stored in fatty tissue. The benefit of fasting is that these chemicals can be eliminated.

After you have fasted you will find your organs have been rejuvenated and your digestion, assimilation, and elimination processes are improved. Many people have also found their sensory powers, with the exception of eyesight, to be more efficient during and right after a fast.

Fasting will renovate, revivify, and purify each of the millions of cells that make up your body.

HISTORY

We mentioned that fasting has a long history. It was employed in caring for the sick in ancient Egypt and Greece.

The Bible mentions fasting many times. Moses fasted for forty days and nights before approaching Mount Sinai to receive the Ten Commandments (Exodus 24: 18, 34:28). Jesus fasted also for forty days and forty nights (Matthew 4:2). Luke, Elijah, and David were practitioners of the fast. The law of Moses sets aside Yom Kippur, the Day of Atonement, as a day of fasting.

Ghandi, who was eighty-four years old when assassinated, fasted frequently. Great men of science and medicine have practiced and extolled the virtues of fasting since the beginning of history.

We are not, of course, suggesting the reader substitute fasting for good medical care. This would be entirely outside of the purpose of a book designed to show rational alternatives to the American way of eating. But there are benefits from fasting and we do not wish to overlook them.

WHAT TO EXPECT FROM FASTING

One of the physiological effects of fasting is body rejuvenation. This is simply the re-energizing of the cells and tissues of the body. Another physiological effect of fasting which may be connected with the first is an increase in the metabolic rate brought about during the fast.

There are some outward improvements you should notice during a fast. Among these is the rejuvenating effect of fasting upon the skin. The color and texture of your skin should improve. As a result you should feel more energetic.

Another way your system is affected by fasting is through a process called autolysis. It is the process of digestion of foods by ferments and enzymes which are generated by the body cells. Autolysis is self-digestion or intra-cellular digestion, and as such it is quite normal for the body. Normal autolysis involves the action of enzymes upon such elements as glycogen, fatty tissue, and bone marrow in preparing these substances for entry into the blood stream. When an abscess rises to the surface of the body to empty itself, autolysis is involved when the flesh between the abscess and the surface is digested by enzymes.

During a fast, your system has the opportunity to redistribute its vital elements, the surpluses and non-vital nutrients being consumed and utilized first. Your assimilative powers are also increased significantly during a fast. You can see this in the improvement of your blood during the fasting period and the rapid assimilation of the food you eat after the fast. This improved assimilation achieved through fasting enables your system to utilize more of its food intake once the fast is completed. This can be very important.

What is actually occurring during a fast is that assimilation is being normalized, whether you assimilated too little or too much of your food intake before the fast. Normalized assimilation means better health and more efficient use of the foods you eat.

A constant diet of defective food and excessive quantities of foods can cause all your organs to weaken. By going on a fast you are giving your body tissues a chance to repair any damage caused in this way. With no new food coming in, your organs can rest and go about the essential process of healing themselves.

One of the most important advantages to be gained by fasting is the physiological rest of every organ which increases elimination. When you are on a fast a good portion of the body energy normally needed to help assimilate new food can be used to expel the accumulations of waste and toxic substances. Decomposing food in the digestive tract is quickly eliminated, and the entire alimentary canal becomes as germ-free and clean of harmful bacteria as is possible for it to be. The body's surplus elements are utilized first. The effusions, dropsical swellings, fat, and infiltrations, are absorbed quite rapidly on a fast.

Due to a greater elimination through the lungs and the skin, you might encounter foul breath and offensive skin odor during the first few days of your fast. Catarrhal eliminations usually increase the first few days, as does the toxicity of urine. In a few cases considerable waste material is lost through vomiting. These symptoms, however, do not always occur while fasting.

During a fast your nervous system and brain also

undergo a physiological rest resulting in a marked improvement of nervous and mental functions.

To summarize the benefits of fasting:

1. It produces rejuvenation of tissues.
2. It induces autolysis of abnormal growths.
3. It speeds up assimilation and elimination.
4. It increases elimination.
5. It allows all of the organs a physiological rest.
6. It promotes nerve energy recuperation.
7. It speeds up the healing process of your body.

Fasting can and often does help the body to rebuild itself. But this is not to say that fasting is some kind of cure-all. It clearly is not. Nor should fasting be considered the only method by which health can be improved. As with everything else, fasting must be judged and utilized rationally.

WHAT A FAST IS AND ISN'T— THE DIFFERENCE BETWEEN FASTING AND STARVATION

There is a difference between fasting and starvation, a very important difference, and it is one which anyone contemplating going on a fast should know well. A fasting person should know the symptoms that signal the end of fasting and the beginning of starvation.

One easy rule that will help you to avoid prolonging your fast into a period of starvation is: avoid setting the length of time for a fast before you start. The time required for a fast to be completed varies from person to person. The length of your fast must be geared to your particular requirements. Some people may exhaust their food reserve in two weeks, while others may take six to eight weeks to reach the same point in their fast. It is at this point, when food reserves are used up, that the fast should be brought to an end. Once the food reserve is depleted, starvation sets in.

One of the factors which makes a difference in the time it takes an individual to deplete his food reserves is the amount of excess fat he carries around. An obese individual will, during a fast, use up the excess fat as additional nourishment.

Some nutritional experts and old-time doctors claim that no fast should be broken until the body reserves are diminished. To support this claim, they point to people who broke their fasts prematurely and were unable to digest the foods they took in. These people vomited everything up. However, while complete fasts might be the ideal they are not always necessary or practical. To avoid any problem, a person coming off a fast of any kind should take only the correct liquid foods. If this is done there should be little problem. We will discuss just what these liquids are later.

Many nutritionists recommend everyone should fast at least one day each week, preferably Sunday. The purpose is to give the system a chance to rest and to clean and rebuild itself. Sunday is the best day for fasting because it is usually not a strenuous day. All exercise should be avoided during a fast, no matter what its length.

A fast should *never* be undertaken without the supervision of your doctor.

ARE FASTS DANGEROUS?

Antagonists of fasting claim that such abstention from food can be dangerous, or even fatal. Some opponents state that fasting weakens the vital organs of the body, especially the heart, and causes the stomach to atrophy, or makes the digestive juices eat away at the walls of the stomach. Others claim fasting produces deficiency disease, tooth decay, lowers the resistance of the body to infection, causes cells to degenerate, promotes edema and acidosis, and in many cases causes death.

Most of these are misconceptions. Many nutritionists believe that fasting, instead of weakening the heart, allows it to rest and gain new strength. Fasting has the same effect on other vital organs, including the stomach and the entire digestive tract. There is no atrophy or impairment whatsoever.

Deficiency ailments are not caused by fasting. If a person's normal day-to-day diet is lacking in some essential vitamins or nutrients, a fast which supplies no additional mineral and vitamins will not worsen the condition. In fact, during a fast, when the system's energy is not used in the functioning of digestion and assimilation, the need for minerals is lowered. Since reserves of these elements in the system are sufficient to meet all needs, no deficiency diseases occur during a fast.

Advocates of fasting insist it is not true that fasting lowers resistance to disease. A fast can, through the processes we discussed, actually increase resistance to disease.

It may well be that the severe critics of fasting are confusing it with starvation, or are looking at people who have gone beyond the point of fasting into a period of starvation. Few people would insist that there is any benefit to be gained from starvation.

It *is* true that during a fast the blood alkalinity is slightly lowered, but this does not ever reach the point of true acidosis, however. There are always sufficient alkaline reserves in the system to defend against this condition during a fast.

Done rationally and under a doctor's observation, fasting can be a safe and practical method of cleansing the system and gaining the benefits of good health.

PREPARING FOR A FAST

Preparing yourself for a fast is not really difficult. Making the decision to fast is probably more difficult than the preparation for it. The one thing you should do is eliminate all concentrated starches from your diet a week before you begin the fast. This can be done best by eating only raw, fresh fruits, vegetables, and juices. By following this advice you will allow your bowels a chance to loosen themselves and promote smooth elimination. Your fast will be much more comfortable and effective if your alimentary canal is clean and free from excessive residues.

THE BEGINNINGS OF THE FAST

During the initial stages of your fast you will probably notice a few discomforts. People are usually very hungry for the first two days. But by the third day the hunger usually abates, with its complete disappearance coming on the fourth or fifth day. There seems to be a marked repugnance for food during the first week of fasting. Some individuals have reported nausea and vomiting at the sight of food. The tongue usually becomes heavily coated and the breath becomes very offensive a few days after the fast has begun.

DURING THE FAST

Bodily reactions during a fast vary significantly from individual to individual. If you fast for an extended period of time, say from six to eight weeks, a marked drop in body temperature will occur. Such a condition should be a warning to you to break the fast immediately. Whenever the body temperature drops rapidly, it is a sign that the system is entering the starvation period.

On occasion a slight chilliness may occur. This chilliness is caused by the decreased cutaneous circulation. It can be countered easily by wearing warmer clothing. The feet also may become cold for the same reason. If this happens, additional socks can be worn.

An erratic pulse is not uncommon and should not concern you unless it becomes persistent and remains very high or very low for more than a few days. If this happens, break the fast.

While people who were very weak at the outset of the fast may experience an increase in strength level, for most individuals strength will diminish. As the fast lengthens, weakness intensifies. Extreme emaciation with weakness to the point of fainting or an inability to walk properly is, of course, an indication to stop the fast.

Many people lose about one pound of weight per day for the first week or two, and then one pound every two or three days thereafter. In extreme cases of obesity, more weight is lost per day, often up to three pounds. This loss of weight is nothing to worry about. The body will regain any weight it needs to reach a normal strength level once the fast is discontinued. Obese people are more likely to experience nausea as the body uses up stored fat, thereby releasing toxic agents such as DDT, which accumulate in the fatty tissues, into the bloodstream.

From the time you have eaten your final meal, the digestive system will become inactive, requiring very little bowel movement. Intestines become empty. This is nothing to worry about, since bowel movement will return to normal right after the fast has ended. If a bowel movement occurs, the action may be either easy or difficult, depending on the type of food which was eaten immediately before the fast began.

There is a pattern of sexual motivation during a fast. In many instances, the desire is either reduced or

101

abolished. Temporary impotence may develop, but like many of the other symptoms we've discussed, it will reverse as soon as the fast has been ended. Many people, including our staff editor-in-chief James Dawson, who fasts often, insist that after a fast their sexual drive returns with renewed vigor. "Nothing in the streets is safe," Dawson was quoted recently, "at least nothing that moves."

Also, it is not uncommon for men who were impotent prior to going on a fast to find they've regained their virility once the fast has ended.

Women who have previously been affected by congestion in the ovaries and uterus may find the menses appearing at irregular intervals while fasting. The menses may appear almost viscid in consistency with an offensive odor. This is the result of a purely natural cleansing of the reproductive system and should not be a cause for alarm.

There are a variety of other irritations which may or may not occur during a fast. These include vomiting, skin eruptions (the body is cleansing itself), slight colds and cramps, backaches, headaches, dizziness, hiccoughs, and sore throats. These symptoms pose no danger and usually disappear in a day or two. Most people do not experience any of these symptoms at all.

TAKING CARE OF YOURSELF WHILE FASTING

During your fast you will require more than your usual amount of rest. An active person consumes his nutritive reserves and energy much more quickly than the individual who takes it easy and doesn't over-exert himself. Proper rest, imporant at any time, will allow you to fast longer and emerge in better condition.

In the advanced stages of fasting you should wear warm clothing. Chilliness will adversely affect the processes of elimination. If you become extremely cold, stop the fast.

Your emotions and mental character play an important role in fasting. You should try to avoid fear and negative thoughts or influences while fasting. Anger, grief, and shock tend to drain your reserve energy and can cause ill effects. If you are under these influences, don't start a fast, and if such influences occur during your fast you should break it off.

When bathing, extremes of temperature should be avoided. The water should be neither too cold nor too hot.

You should drink about a quart of water a day during your fast. Some people recommend several quarts of water a day; others advocate fasting without water altogether. These extremes should be avoided. Experience shows us that either can prove harmful, if not fatal, during fasting. Thirst can be a reliable guide. Try to drink a 4 to 6 ounce glass of water every few hours, even if you do not feel a great need for it.

Many old-timers will tell you that you need an enema while fasting. Once more, experience counters such advice. You should refrain from using an enema at all during a fast. Advocates of the enema argue that toxins and waste matter are being deposited in the colon and reabsorbed into the blood. Cleansing the bowel with an enema each day is supposed to prevent this reabsorption.

The facts of the matter are quite different. The colon is not fundamentally an organ in which much absorption occurs, and the entire alimentary canal, including the colon, becomes free of all morbid waste during the fast. No substantial evidence proves otherwise. The use of an enema would cause an additional drain on the individual's vitality, wash away the mucus which normally protects the lining of the colon, and break some of the tiny muscles of the intestinal wall, causing the muscle tone to be impaired.

Do not take drugs while fasting. Any drugs taken will be quickly absorbed into the system and usually cause adverse effects. This includes serums and injections of any kind.

BREAKING YOUR FAST

If your fast is not ended properly, the results will often be unfavorable. When the intake of food is stopped, the system adjusts itself to this new condition. The digestive organs cease to exercise their natural functions, the digestive glands no longer produce the usual juices, and the stomach shrinks to less than its normal size. All of these reactions are part of the physiological rest.

It only takes a few days for your system to lose its natural ability to digest and assimilate food in its normal manner. Since your system cannot immediately adjust and regain all its normal digestive power when the fast ends, it must be given time to readjust. Therefore, if your first intake of food is heavy or concentrated, difficulty will occur and the food will very likely be vomited up. Even if no vomiting occurs, the food will not be normally digested and will decay and ferment, causing distress, discomfort, and excessive gas. These reactions can be quite serious if the decay and fermentation occur in the lower section of the digestive tract in the small intestine.

Because of the possibility of such problems, you should first drink liquids. Liquid, quickly absorbed and easily digested, is more soothing and less abrasive to the delicate mucus membrane of the stomach than concentrated foods. The recommended liquids are fruit and vegetable juices or broths. Many practitioners prefer unstrained orange juice when breaking a fast.

To end your fast, drink one half glass of juice. Follow this with one half glass of juice every hour, or one glass every two hours. On the second day, follow the same schedule. After that, the amount of juice can be increased. Do not take more than one pint of juice at one sitting after a fast.

The juices you take should not be cold or iced. They should be sipped very slowly to allow them to be "chewed" in the mouth before being swallowed. In this way, the acid and sugar of the fruit mixes with saliva and the work of the stomach is reduced. Drinking the juice too quickly or drinking it when it is too cold can produce stomach cramps.

LENGTH OF JUICE DIET AFTER A FAST

You should maintain your juice diet for about six days when coming off a fast. The ratio of fasts to juice diet may be only two or three to one in the case of very short fasts. It becomes four or five to one for moderate fasts, and seven to one for longer fasts. Below is a list that will suggest a time schedule for correlating the juice diet with the length of your fast.

Length of Fast	Length of Juice Diet
1-3 days	1 day
4-8 days	2 days
9-15 days	3 days
16-24 days	4 days
25-25 days	5 days
over 35 days	6 days

After you have been on the juice diet for the recommended length of time, you can eat any form of uncooked food. On successive days the quantity of food can be gradually increased. It is important that you not try to eat large meals to compensate for previous restriction. Moderate eating habits are the safest and healthiest.

Fasting is not a cure-all. You should not feel a successful fast has made you immune to illness or disease. Your insurance against ailments is to live properly. It's that simple. A fast should be part of a total health program geared to your particular needs. It will do you little good to go off a fast and eat inadequately. So to preserve good health you must control your eating habits. Fasting is a means of promoting the remedy of illness and creation of health, not a method of maintaining health. An adequate and rational diet, which is what this whole book has been about, should do that. The choice to eat rationally or irrationally is yours. A book can do no more than offer guides. It is our hope that this book will help you in eating a rational diet and maintaining good health throughout your life.

CHAPTER SIX

FOOD VALUE TABLES

The following tables can be used by the reader in determining the precise food values of nearly 500 food items commonly used in the United States. The values are based on data from the U.S. Department of Agriculture. With the use of these charts it should be easy for the reader to plan his daily menu to include all the nutritional elements necessary for good health.

This information is broken down into two tables. The first covers The Nutritive Values of the Edible Part of Foods. The second is a compilation of The Amino Acid Content of Foods. This table gives you the average amounts of the eight "essential" amino acids found in each food, plus arginine and histidine.

NUTRITIVE VALUES OF THE EDIBLE PART OF FOODS

Reprinted from *Nutritive Value of Foods* (U.S. Department of Agriculture, Home and Garden Bulletin No. 72).

[Dashes show that no basis could be found for imputing a value although there was some reason to believe that a measurable amount of the constituent might be present]

Food, Approximate Measure, and Weight (in Grams)	Grams	Food Energy	Protein	Fat (Total Lipid)	Fatty acids Saturated (Total)	Fatty acids Unsaturated Oleic	Fatty acids Unsaturated Linoleic	Carbohydrate	Calcium	Iron	Vitamin A Value	Thiamine	Riboflavin	Niacin	Ascorbic Acid
		(Calories)	(Gm.)	(Gm.)	(Gm.)	(Gm.)	(Gm.)	(Gm.)	(Mo.)	(Mo.)	(I.U.)	(Mo.)	(Mo.)	(Mo.)	(Mo.)
MILK, CREAM, CHEESE; RELATED PRODUCTS															
Milk, cow's:															
Fluid, whole (3.5% fat), 1 cup	244	160	9	9	5	3	Trace	12	288	0.1	350	0.08	0.42	0.1	2
Fluid, nonfat (skim), 1 cup	246	90	9	Trace	—	—	—	13	298	.1	10	.10	.44	.2	2
Buttermilk, cultured, from skim milk, 1 cup	246	90	9	Trace	—	—	—	13	298	.1	10	.09	.44	.2	2
Evaporated, unsweetened, undiluted, 1 cup	252	345	18	20	11	7	1	24	635	.3	820	.10	.84	.5	3
Condensed, sweetened, undiluted, 1 cup	306	980	25	27	15	9	1	166	802	.3	1,090	.23	1.17	.5	3
Dry, whole, 1 cup	103	515	27	28	16	9	1	39	936	.5	1,160	.30	1.50	.7	6
Dry, nonfat, instant, 1 cup	70	250	25	Trace	—	—	—	36	905	.4	20	.24	1.25	.6	5
Milk, goat's:															
Fluid, whole, 1 cup	244	165	8	10	6	2	Trace	11	315	.2	390	.10	.27	.7	2

Cream:

Half-and-half (cream and milk).															
1 cup	242	325	8	28	16	9	1	11	261	.1	1,160	.08	.38	.1	2
1 tablespoon	15	20	Trace	2	1	1	Trace	1	16	Trace	70	Trace	.02	Trace	Trace
Light, coffee or table															
1 cup	240	505	7	49	27	16	1	10	245	.1	2,030	.07	.36	.1	2
1 tablespoon	15	30	Trace	3	2	1	Trace	1	15	Trace	130	Trace	.02	Trace	Trace
Whipping, unwhipped (volume about double when whipped):															
Light															
1 cup	239	715	6	75	41	25	2	9	203	.1	3,070	.06	.30	.1	2
1 tablespoon	15	45	Trace	5	3	2	Trace	1	13	Trace	190	Trace	.02	Trace	Trace
Heavy															
1 cup	238	840	5	89	49	29	3	7	178	.1	3,670	.05	.26	.1	2
Cheese:															
Blue or Roquefort type															
1 ounce	28	105	6	9	5	3	Trace	1	89	.1	350	.01	.17	.1	0
Cheddar or American:															
Ungrated															
1 inch cube	17	70	4	5	3	2	Trace	1	128	.2	220	Trace	.08	Trace	0
Grated															
1 cup	112	445	28	36	20	12	1	2	840	1.1	1,470	.03	.51	.1	0
1 tablespoon	7	30	2	2	1	1	Trace	Trace	52	.1	90	Trace	.03	Trace	0
Cheddar, process															
1 ounce	28	105	7	9	5	3	Trace	1	219	.3	350	Trace	.12	Trace	0
Cheese foods, Cheddar															
1 ounce	28	90	6	7	4	2	Trace	2	162	.2	280	.01	.16	Trace	0
Cottage cheese, from skim milk:															
Creamed															
1 cup	225	240	31	9	5	3	Trace	7	212	0.7	380	0.07	0.56	0.2	0
1 ounce	28	30	4	1	1	Trace	Trace	1	27	.1	50	.01	.07	Trace	0
Uncreamed															
1 cup	225	195	38	1	Trace	Trace	---	6	202	.9	20	.07	.63	.2	0
1 ounce	28	25	5	Trace	---	---	---	1	26	.1	Trace	.01	.08	Trace	0
Cream cheese															
1 ounce	28	105	2	11	6	4	Trace	1	18	.1	440	Trace	.07	Trace	0
1 tablespoon	15	55	1	6	3	2	Trace	Trace	9	Trace	230	Trace	.04	Trace	0

Food, Approximate Measure, and Weight (in Grams)	Grams	Food Energy (Calories)	Protein (Gm.)	Fat (Total Lipid) (Gm.)	Fatty acids Saturated (Total) (Gm.)	Unsaturated Oleic (Gm.)	Linoleic (Gm.)	Carbohydrate (Gm.)	Calcium (Mo.)	Iron (Mo.)	Vitamin A Value (I.U.)	Thiamine (Mo.)	Riboflavin (Mo.)	Niacin (Mo.)	Ascorbic Acid (Mo.)
CHEESE Swiss (domestic) 1 ounce	28	105	8	8	4	3	Trace	1	262	.3	320	Trace	.11	Trace	0
Milk beverages: Cocoa 1 cup	242	235	9	11	6	4	Trace	26	286	.9	390	.09	.45	.4	2
Chocolate-flavored milk drink (made with skim milk). 1 cup	250	190	8	6	3	2	Trace	27	270	.4	210	.09	.41	.2	2
Malted milk 1 cup	270	280	13	12	----	----	----	32	364	.8	670	.17	.56	.2	2
Milk desserts: Cornstarch pudding, plain (blanc mange). 1 cup	248	275	9	10	5	3	Trace	39	290	.1	390	.07	.40	.1	2
Custard, baked 1 cup	248	285	13	14	6	5	1	28	278	1.0	870	.10	.47	.2	1
Ice cream, plain, factory packed: Slice or cut brick, 1/8 of quart brick. 1 slice or cut brick	71	145	3	9	5	3	Trace	15	87	.1	370	.03	.13	.1	1
Container 3½ fluid ounces	62	130	2	8	4	3	Trace	13	76	.1	320	.03	.12	.1	1
Container 8 fluid ounces	142	295	6	18	10	6	1	28	175	.1	740	.06	.27	.1	1
Ice milk 1 cup	187	285	9	10	6	3	Trace	42	292	.2	390	.09	.41	.2	2
Yoghurt, from partially skimmed milk. 1 cup	246	120	8	4	2	1	Trace	13	295	.1	170	.09	.43	.2	2

EGGS

Eggs, large, 24 ounces per dozen:

Food															
Raw:															
1 egg — Whole, without shell	50	80	6	6	2	3	Trace	Trace	27	1.1	590	.05	.15	Trace	0
1 white — White of egg	33	15	4	Trace	---	---	---	Trace	3	Trace	0	Trace	.09	Trace	0
1 yolk — Yolk of egg	17	60	3	5	2	2	Trace	Trace	24	.9	580	.04	.07	Trace	0
Cooked:															
2 eggs — Boiled, shell removed	100	160	13	12	4	5	1	1	54	2.3	1,180	.09	.28	.1	0
1 egg — Scrambled, with milk and fat	64	110	7	8	3	3	Trace	Trace	51	1.1	690	.05	.18	Trace	0

MEAT, POULTRY, FISH, SHELLFISH; RELATED PRODUCTS

Food															
Bacon, broiled or fried, crisp, 2 slices	16	100	5	8	3	4	1	1	2	.5	0	.08	.05	.8	---
Beef, trimmed to retail basis,[1] cooked:															
Cuts braised, simmered, or pot-roasted:															
Lean and fat 3 ounces	85	245	23	16	8	7	Trace	0	10	2.9	30	.04	.18	3.5	---
Lean only 2.5 ounces	72	140	22	5	2	2	Trace	0	10	2.7	10	.04	.16	3.3	---
Hamburger (ground beef), broiled:															
Lean 3 ounces	85	185	23	10	5	4	Trace	0	10	3.0	20	.08	.20	5.1	---
Regular 3 ounces	85	245	21	17	8	8	Trace	0	9	2.7	30	.07	.18	4.6	---
Roast, oven-cooked, no liquid added:															
Relatively fat, such as rib:															
Lean and fat 3 ounces	85	375	17	34	16	15	1	0	8	2.2	70	.05	.13	3.1	---
Lean only 1.8 ounces	51	125	14	7	3	3	Trace	0	6	1.8	10	.04	.11	2.6	---

[1]Outer layer of fat on the cut was removed to within approximately ½ inch of the lean. Deposits of fat within the cut were not removed.

Food, Approximate Measure, and Weight (in Grams)	Grams	Food Energy (Calories)	Protein (Gm.)	Fat (Total Lipid) (Gm.)	Fatty acids Saturated (Total) (Gm.)	Unsaturated Oleic (Gm.)	Unsaturated Linoleic (Gm.)	Carbohydrate (Gm.)	Calcium (Mg.)	Iron (Mg.)	Vitamin A Value (I.U.)	Thiamine (Mg.)	Riboflavin (Mg.)	Niacin (Mg.)	Ascorbic Acid (Mg.)
Relatively lean, such as heel of round:															
Lean and fat 3 ounces	85	165	25	7	3	3	Trace	0	11	3.2	10	.06	.19	4.5	---
Lean only 2.7 ounces	78	125	24	3	1	1	Trace	0	10	3.0	Trace	.06	.18	4.3	---
Steak, broiled:															
Relatively fat, such as sirloin:															
Lean and fat 3 ounces	85	330	20	27	13	12	1	0	9	2.5	50	.05	.16	4.0	---
Lean only 2.0 ounces	56	115	18	4	2	2	Trace	0	7	2.2	10	.05	.14	3.6	---
Relatively lean, such as round:															
Lean and fat 3 ounces	85	220	24	13	6	6	Trace	0	10	3.0	20	.07	.19	4.8	---
Lean only 2.4 ounces	68	130	21	4	2	2	Trace	0	9	2.5	10	.06	.16	4.1	---
Beef, canned:															
Corned beef 3 ounces	85	185	22	10	5	4	Trace	0	17	3.7	20	.01	.20	2.9	---
Corned beef hash 3 ounces	85	155	7	10	5	4	Trace	9	11	1.7	---	.01	.08	1.8	---
Beef, dried or chipped 2 ounces	57	115	19	4	2	2	Trace	0	11	2.9	---	.04	.18	2.2	---
Beef and vegetable stew 1 cup	235	210	15	10	5	4	Trace	15	28	2.8	2,310	.13	.17	4.4	15
Beef potpie, baked: Individual pie, 4¼-inch diameter, weight before															

Food	grams	calories													
baking about 8 ounces. 1 pie	227	560	23	33	9	20	2	43	32	4.1	1,860	.25	.27	4.5	7
Chicken, cooked: Flesh only, broiled 3 ounces	85	115	20	3	1	1	1	0	8	1.4	80	0.05	0.16	7.4	---
Breast, fried, ½ breast: With bone 3.3 ounces	94	155	25	5	1	2	1	1	9	1.3	70	.04	.17	11.2	---
Flesh and skin only 2.7 ounces	76	155	25	5	1	2	1	1	9	1.3	70	.04	.17	11.2	---
Drumstick, fried: With bone 2.1 ounces	59	90	12	4	1	2	1	Trace	6	.9	50	.03	.15	2.7	---
Flesh and skin only 1.3 ounces	38	90	12	4	1	2	1	Trace	6	.9	50	.03	.15	2.7	---
Chicken, canned, boneless 3 ounces	85	170	18	10	3	4	2	0	18	1.3	200	.03	.11	3.7	3
Chicken potpie, See Poultry potpie.															
Chile con carne, canned: With beans 1 cup	250	335	19	15	7	7	Trace	30	80	4.2	150	.08	.18	3.2	---
Without beans 1 cup	255	510	26	38	18	17	1	15	97	3.6	380	.05	.31	5.6	---
Heart, beef, lean, braised 3 ounces	85	160	27	5	---	---	---	1	5	5.0	20	.21	1.04	6.5	1
Lamb, trimmed to retail basis,[1] cooked: Chop, thick, with bone, broiled. 1 chop, 4.8 ounces	137	400	25	33	18	12	1	0	10	1.5	---	.14	.25	5.6	---
Lean and fat 4.0 ounces	112	400	25	33	18	12	1	0	10	1.5	---	.14	.25	5.6	---
Lean only 2.6 ounces	74	140	21	6	3	2	Trace	0	9	1.5	---	.11	.20	4.5	---
Leg, roasted: Lean and fat 3 ounces	85	235	22	16	9	6	Trace	0	9	1.4	---	.13	.23	4.7	---
Lean only 2.5 ounces	71	130	20	5	3	2	Trace	0	9	1.4	---	.12	.21	4.4	---

113

Food, Approximate Measure, and Weight (in Grams)	Grams	Food Energy (Calories)	Protein (Gm.)	Fat (Total Lipid) (Gm.)	Fatty acids			Carbohydrate (Gm.)	Calcium (Mg.)	Iron (Mg.)	Vitamin A Value (I.U.)	Thiamine (Mg.)	Riboflavin (Mg.)	Niacin (Mg.)	Ascorbic Acid (Mg.)
					Saturated (Total) (Gm.)	Unsaturated Oleic (Gm.)	Unsaturated Linoleic (Gm.)								
Shoulder, roasted:															
Lean and fat															
3 ounces	85	285	18	23	13	8	1	0	9	1.0	---	.11	.20	4.0	---
Lean only															
2.3 ounces	64	130	17	6	3	2	Trace	0	8	1.0	---	.10	.18	3.7	---
Liver, beef, fried															
2 ounces	57	130	15	6	---	---	---	3	6	5.0	30,280	.15	2.37	9.4	15
Pork, cured, cooked:															
Ham, light cure, lean and fat, roasted.															
3 ounces	85	245	18	19	7	8	2	0	8	2.2	0	.40	.16	3.1	---
Luncheon meat:															
Boiled ham, sliced															
2 ounces	57	135	11	10	4	4	1	0	6	1.6	0	.25	.09	1.5	---
Canned, spiced or unspiced,															
2 ounces	57	165	8	14	5	6	1	1	5	1.2	0	.18	.12	1.6	---
Pork, fresh, trimmed to retail basis,[1] cooked:															
Chop, thick, with bone															
1 chop, 3.5 ounces	98	260	16	21	8	9	2	0	8	2.2	0	.63	.18	3.8	---
Lean and fat															
2.3 ounces	66	260	16	21	8	9	2	0	8	2.2	0	.63	.18	3.8	---
Lean only															
1.7 ounces	48	130	15	7	2	3	1	0	7	1.9	0	.54	.16	3.3	---
Roast, oven-cooked, no liquid added:															
Lean and fat															

[1]Outer layer of fat on the cut was removed to within approximately ½ inch of the lean. Deposits of fat within the cut were not removed.

3 ounces	85	310	21	24	9	10	2	0	9	2.7	0	.78	.22	4.7	—
Lean only — 2.4 ounces	68	175	20	10	3	4	1	0	9	2.6	0	.73	.21	4.4	—
Cuts, simmered:															
Lean and fat — 3 ounces	85	320	20	26	9	11	2	0	8	2.5	0	.46	.21	4.1	—
Lean only — 2.2 ounces	63	135	18	6	2	3	1	0	8	2.3	0	.42	.19	3.7	—
Poultry potpie (based on chicken potpie). Individual pie, 4¼-inch diameter, weight before baking, about — 1 pie	227	535	23	31	10	15	3	42	68	3.0	3,020	.25	.26	4.1	5
Sausage:															
Bologna, slice, 4.1 by 0.1 inch. 8 slices	227	690	27	62	—	—	—	2	16	4.1	—	.36	.49	6.0	—
Frankfurter, cooked — 1 frankfurter	51	155	6	14	—	—	—	1	3	.8	—	.08	.10	1.3	—
Pork, links or patty, cooked. 4 ounces	113	540	21	50	18	21	5	Trace	8	2.7	0	.89	.39	4.2	—
Tongue, beef, braised — 3 ounces	85	210	18	14	—	—	—	Trace	6	1.9	—	.04	.25	3.0	—
Turkey potpie. See Poultry potpie.															
Veal, cooked:															
Cutlet, without bone, broiled. 3 ounces	85	185	23	9	5	4	Trace	—	9	2.7	—	.06	.21	4.6	—
Roast, medium fat, medium done; lean and fat. 3 ounces	85	230	23	14	7	6	Trace	0	10	2.9	—	.11	.26	6.6	—
Fish and shellfish:															
Bluefish, baked or broiled. 3 ounces	85	135	22	4	—	—	—	0	25	.6	40	.09	.08	1.6	—
Clams:															
Raw, meat only — 3 ounces	85	65	11	1	—	—	—	2	59	5.2	90	.08	.15	1.1	8
Canned, solids and liquid. 3 ounces	85	45	7	1	—	—	—	2	47	3.5	—	.01	.09	.9	—
Crabmeat, canned — 3 ounces	85	85	15	2	—	—	—	1	38	.7	—	.07	.07	1.6	—

Food, Approximate Measure, and Weight (in Grams)	Grams	Food Energy (Calories)	Protein (Gm.)	Fat (Total Lipid) (Gm.)	Fatty acids Saturated (Total) (Gm.)	Fatty acids Unsaturated Oleic (Gm.)	Fatty acids Unsaturated Linoleic (Gm.)	Carbohydrate (Gm.)	Calcium (Mo.)	Iron (Mo.)	Vitamin A Value (I.U.)	Thiamine (Mo.)	Riboflavin (Mo.)	Niacin (Mo.)	Ascorbic Acid (Mo.)
Fish sticks, breaded, cooked, frozen; stick, 3.8 by 1.0 by 0.5 inch. 10 sticks or 8-ounce package	227	400	38	20	5	4	10	15	25	.9	---	.09	.16	3.6	---
Fish and shellfish—Continued Haddock, fried 3 ounces	85	140	17	5	1	3	---	5	34	1.0	---	0.03	0.06	2.7	2
Mackerel: Broiled, Atlantic 3 ounces	85	200	19	13	---	---	---	0	5	1.0	450	.13	.23	6.5	---
Canned, Pacific, solids and liquid.[2]	85							0	221	1.9	20	.02	.27	7.4	---
Ocean perch, breaded (egg and breadcrumbs), fried. 3 ounces	85	195	16	11	---	---	---	6	28	1.1	---	.08	.09	1.5	---
Oysters, meat only: Raw, 13-19 medium selects. 1 cup	240	160	20	4	---	---	---	8	226	13.2	740	.33	.43	6.0	---
Oyster stew, 1 part oysters to 3 parts milk by volume, 3-4 oysters. 1 cup	230	200	11	12	---	---	---	11	269	3.3	640	.13	.41	1.6	---
Salmon, pink, canned 3 ounces	85	120	17	5	1	1	Trace	0	[3]167	.7	60	.03	.16	6.8	---
Sardines, Atlantic, canned in oil, drained solids. 3 ounces	85	175	20	9	---	---	---	0	372	2.5	190	.02	.17	4.6	---

[2]Vitamin values based on drained solids. If bones are discarded, value will be greatly reduced.

[3]Based on total contents of can.

Food														
Shad, baked, 3 ounces	85	170	20	10	---	---	---	0	20	.5	20	.11	.22	7.3	---
Shrimp, canned, meat only. 3 ounces	85	100	21	1	---	---	---	1	98	2.6	50	.01	.03	1.5	---
Swordfish, broiled with butter or margarine. 3 ounces	85	150	24	5	---	---	---	0	23	1.1	1,750	.03	.04	9.3	---
Tuna, canned in oil, drained solids. 3 ounces	85	170	24	7	---	---	---	0	7	1.6	70	.04	.10	10.1	---
Almonds, shelled 1 cup	142	850	26	77	6	52	15	28	332	6.7	0	.34	1.31	5.0	Trace
Beans, dry:														
Common varieties, such as Great Northern, navy, and others, canned:														
Red 1 cup	256	230	15	1	---	---	---	42	74	4.6	Trace	.13	.10	1.5	---
White, with tomato sauce:														
With pork 1 cup	261	320	16	7	3	3	1	50	141	4.7	340	.20	.08	1.5	5
Without pork 1 cup	261	310	16	1	---	---	---	60	177	5.2	160	.18	.09	1.5	5
Lima, cooked 1 cup	192	260	16	1	---	---	---	48	56	5.6	Trace	.26	.12	1.3	Trace
Brazil nuts 1 cup	140	915	20	94	19	45	24	15	260	4.8	Trace	1.34	.17	2.2	---
Cashew nuts, roasted 1 cup	135	760	23	62	10	43	4	40	51	5.1	140	.58	.33	2.4	---
Coconut:														
Fresh, shredded 1 cup	97	335	3	34	29	2	Trace	9	13	1.6	0	.05	.02	.5	3
Dried, shredded, sweetened. 1 cup	62	340	2	24	21	2	Trace	33	10	1.2	0	.02	.02	.2	0
Cowpeas or blackeye peas, dry, cooked. 1 cup	248	190	13	1	---	---	---	34	42	3.2	20	.41	.11	1.1	Trace
Peanuts, roasted, salted:														
Halves 1 cup	144	840	37	72	16	31	21	27	107	3.0	---	.46	.19	24.7	0
Chopped 1 tablespoon	9	55	2	5	1	2	1	2	7	.2	---	.03	.01	1.5	0

Food, Approximate Measure, and Weight (in Grams)	Grams	Food Energy (Calories)	Protein (Gm.)	Fat (Total Lipid) (Gm.)	Fatty acids Saturated (Total) (Gm.)	Unsaturated Oleic (Gm.)	Linoleic (Gm.)	Carbohydrate (Gm.)	Calcium (Mg.)	Iron (Mg.)	Vitamin A Value (I.U.)	Thiamine (Mg.)	Riboflavin (Mg.)	Niacin (Mg.)	Ascorbic Acid (Mg.)
Peanut butter 1 tablespoon	16	95	4	8	2	4	2	3	9	.3	---	.02	.02	2.4	0
Peas, split, dry, cooked 1 cup	250	290	20	1	---	---	---	52	28	4.2	100	.37	.22	2.2	---
Pecans:															
Halves 1 cup	108	740	10	77	5	48	15	16	79	2.6	140	.93	.14	1.0	2
Chopped 1 tablespoon	7.5	50	1	5	Trace	3	1	1	5	.2	10	.06	.01	.1	Trace
Walnuts, shelled:															
Black or native, chopped. 1 cup	126	790	26	75	4	26	36	19	Trace	7.6	380	.28	.14	.9	---
English or Persian:															
Halves 1 cup	100	650	15	64	4	10	40	16	99	3.1	30	.33	.13	.9	3
Chopped 1 tablespoon	8	50	1	5	Trace	1	3	1	8	.2	Trace	.03	.01	.1	Trace
VEGETABLES AND VEGETABLE PRODUCTS															
Asparagus:															
Cooked, cut spears 1 cup	175	35	4	Trace	---	---	---	6	37	1.0	1,580	.27	.32	2.4	46
Canned spears, medium:															
Green 6 spears	96	20	2	Trace	---	---	---	3	18	1.8	770	.06	.10	.8	14
Bleached 6 spears	96	20	2	Trace	---	---	---	4	15	1.0	80	.05	.06	.7	14

Food	Measure														
Beans:															
Lima, Immature, cooked	1 cup	160	180	12	1	—	—	—	32	75	4.0	450	.29	.16	2.0	28
Snap, green:															
Cooked:															
In small amount of water, short time.	1 cup	125	30	2	Trace	—	—	—	7	62	.8	680	.08	.11	.6	16
In large amount of water, long time.	1 cup	125	30	2	Trace	—	—	—	7	62	0.8	680	0.07	0.10	0.4	13
Canned: Solids and liquid	1 cup	239	45	2	Trace	—	—	—	10	81	2.9	690	.08	.10	.7	9
Strained or chopped (baby food),	1 ounce	28	5	Trace	Trace	—	—	—	1	9	.3	110	.01	.02	.1	Trace
Bean sprouts. See Sprouts.															
Beets, cooked, diced	1 cup	165	50	2	Trace	—	—	—	12	23	.8	40	.04	.07	.5	11
Broccoli spears, cooked	1 cup	150	40	5	Trace	—	—	—	7	132	1.2	3,750	.14	.29	1.2	135
Brussels sprouts, cooked	1 cup	130	45	5	1	—	—	—								
Cabbage:															
Raw: Finely shredded	1 cup	100	25	1	Trace		2			9	52	.5	180	.06	.06	.3	35
Coleslaw	1 cup	120	120	1	9	2	2	5	5	49	.4	130	.05	.05	.3	47
Cooked:															
In small amount of water, short time.	1 cup	170	35	2	Trace	—	—	—	7	75	.5	220	.07	.07	.5	56
In large amount of water, long time.	1 cup	170	30	2	Trace	—	—	—	7	71	.5	200	.04	.04	.2	40

Food, Approximate Measure, and Weight (in Grams)	Grams	Food Energy	Protein	Fat (Total Lipid)	Fatty acids Saturated (Total)	Unsaturated Oleic	Linoleic	Carbohydrate	Calcium	Iron	Vitamin A Value	Thiamine	Riboflavin	Niacin	Ascorbic Acid
	Grams	(Calories)	(Gm.)	(Gm.)	(Gm.)	(Gm.)	(Gm.)	(Gm.)	(Mo.)	(Mo.)	(I.U.)	(Mo.)	(Mo.)	(Mo.)	(Mo.)
Cabbage, celery or Chinese:															
Raw, leaves and stalk, 1-inch pieces. 1 cup	100	15	1	Trace	—	—	—	3	43	.6	150	.05	.04	.6	25
Cabbage, spoon (or pakchoy), cooked. 1 cup	150	20	2	Trace	—	—	—	4	222	.9	4,650	.07	.12	1.1	23
Carrots:															
Raw:															
Whole, 5½ by 1-inch, (25 thin strips), 1 carrot	50	20	1	Trace	—	—	—	5	18	.4	5,500	.03	.03	.3	4
Grated 1 cup	110	45	1	Trace	—	—	—	11	41	.8	12,100	.06	.06	.7	9
Cooked, diced 1 cup	145	45	1	Trace	—	—	—	10	49	.9	15,220	.08	.07	.7	9
Canned, strained or chopped (baby food), 1 ounce	28	10	Trace	Trace	—	—	—	2	7	.1	3,690	.01	.01	.1	1
Cauliflower, cooked, flowerbuds. 1 cup	120	25	3	Trace	—	—	—	5	25	.8	70	.11	.10	.7	66
Celery, raw:															
Stalk, large outer, 8 by about 1½ inches, at root end. 1 stalk	40	5	Trace	Trace	—	—	—	2	16	.1	100	.01	.01	.1	4
Pieces, diced 1 cup	100	15	1	Trace	—	—	—	4	39	.3	240	.03	.03	.3	9
Collards, cooked 1 cup	190	55	5	1	—	—	—	9	289	1.1	10,260	.27	.37	2.4	87
Corn, sweet:															

Food	Measure	Weight (g)	Food energy	Protein	Fat	Fatty acids	Carbohydrate	Calcium	Iron	Vitamin A	Thiamine	Riboflavin	Niacin	Ascorbic acid
Cooked, ear 5 by 1¾ inches.[a]	1 ear	140	70	3	1	—	16	2	.5	[b]310	.09	.08	1.0	7
Canned, solids and liquid.	1 cup	256	170	5	2	—	40	10	1.0	[b]690	.07	.12	2.3	13
Cowpeas, cooked, immature seeds.	1 cup	160	175	13	1	—	29	38	3.4	560	.49	.18	2.3	28
Cucumbers, 10-ounce; 7½ by about 2 inches: Raw, pared	1 cucumber	207	30	1	Trace	—	7	35	.6	Trace	.07	.09	.4	23
Raw, pared, center slice ⅛-inch thick.	6 slices	50	5	Trace	Trace	—	2	8	.2	Trace	.02	.02	.1	6
Dandelion greens, cooked.	1 cup	180	60	4	1	—	12	252	3.2	21,060	.24	.29	—	32
Endive, curly (including escarole).	2 ounces	57	10	1	Trace	—	2	46	1.0	1,870	.04	.08	.3	6
Kale, leaves including stems, cooked.	1 cup	110	30	4	1	—	4	147	1.3	8,140	—	—	—	68
Lettuce, raw: Butterhead, as Boston types; head, 4-inch diameter.	1 head	220	30	3	Trace	—	6	77	4.4	2,130	.14	.13	.6	18
Crisphead, as Iceberg; head, 4¾-inch diameter.	1 head	454	60	4	Trace	—	13	91	2.3	1,500	.29	.27	1.3	29
Looseleaf, or bunching varieties, leaves.	2 large	50	10	1	Trace	—	2	34	.7	950	.03	.04	.2	9
Mushrooms, canned, solids and liquid.	1 cup	244	40	5	Trace	—	6	15	1.2	Trace	.04	.60	4.8	4
Mustard greens, cooked	1 cup	140	35	3	1	—	6	193	2.5	8,120	.11	.19	.9	68
Okra, cooked, pod 3 by ⅝-inch.	8 pods	85	25	2	Trace	—	5	78	.4	420	.11	.15	.8	17

[a] Measure and weight apply to entire vegetable or fruit including parts not usually eaten.

[b] Based on yellow varieties; white varieties contain only a trace of cryptoxanthin and carotenes, the pigments in corn that have biological activity.

Food, Approximate Measure, and Weight (in Grams)	Grams	Food Energy (Calories)	Protein (Gm.)	Fat (Total Lipid) (Gm.)	Fatty acids Saturated (Total) (Gm.)	Fatty acids Unsaturated Oleic (Gm.)	Fatty acids Unsaturated Linoleic (Gm.)	Carbohydrate (Gm.)	Calcium (Mg.)	Iron (Mg.)	Vitamin A Value (I.U.)	Thiamine (Mg.)	Riboflavin (Mg.)	Niacin (Mg.)	Ascorbic Acid (Mg.)
VEGETABLES AND VEGETABLE PRODUCTS—Continued															
Onions:															
Mature:															
Raw, onion 2½-inch diameter. 1 onion	110	40	2	Trace	---	---	---	10	30	0.6	40	0.04	0.04	0.2	11
Cooked 1 cup	210	60	3	Trace	---	---	---	14	50	.8	80	.06	.06	.4	14
Young green, small, without tops. 6 onions	50	20	1	Trace	---	---	---	5	20	.3	Trace	.02	.02	.2	12
Parsley, raw, chopped 1 tablespoon	3.5	1	Trace	Trace	---	---	---	Trace	7	.2	300	Trace	.01	Trace	6
Parsnips, cooked 1 cup	155	100	2	1	---	---	---	23	70	.9	50	.11	.13	.2	16
Peas, green:															
Cooked 1 cup	160	115	9	1	---	---	---	19	37	2.9	860	.44	.17	3.7	33
Canned, solids and liquid. 1 cup	249	165	9	1	---	---	---	31	50	4.2	1,120	.23	.13	2.2	22
Canned, strained (baby food), 1 ounce	28	15	1	Trace	---	---	---	3	3	.4	140	.02	.02	.4	3
Peppers, hot, red, without seeds, dried (ground chili powder, added seasonings). 1 tablespoon	15	50	2	2	---	---	---	8	40	2.3	9,750	.03	.17	1.3	2
Peppers, sweet:															
Raw, medium, about 6 per pound:															

Food	Grams	Calories												
Green pod without stem and seeds.														
1 pod	62	15	1	Trace	---	---	3	6	.4	260	.05	.05	.3	79
Red pod without stem and seeds.														
1 pod	60	20	1	Trace	---	---	4	8	.4	2,670	.05	.05	.3	122
Canned, pimientos, medium.														
1 pod	38	10	Trace	Trace	---	---	2	3	.6	870	.01	.02	.1	36
Potatoes, medium (about 3 per pound raw):														
Baked, peeled after baking.														
1 potato	99	90	3	Trace	---	---	21	9	.7	Trace	.10	.04	1.7	20
Boiled:														
Peeled after boiling														
1 potato	136	105	3	Trace	---	---	23	10	.8	Trace	.13	.05	2.0	22
Peeled before boiling														
1 potato	122	80	2	Trace	---	---	18	7	.6	Trace	.11	.04	1.4	20
French-fried, piece 2 by ½ by ½-inch:														
Cooked in deep fat														
10 pieces	57	155	2	7	2	4	20	9	.7	Trace	.07	.04	1.8	12
Frozen, heated														
10 pieces	57	125	2	5	1	2	19	5	1.0	Trace	.08	.01	1.5	12
Mashed:														
Milk added														
1 cup	195	125	4	1	---	---	25	47	.8	50	.16	.10	2.0	19
Milk and butter added.														
1 cup	195	185	4	8	4	Trace	24	47	.8	330	.16	.10	1.9	18
Potato chips, medium, 2-inch diameter.														
10 chips	20	115	1	8	2	4	10	8	.4	Trace	.04	.01	1.0	3
Pumpkin, canned														
1 cup	228	75	2	1	---	---	18	57	.9	14,590	.07	.12	1.3	12
Radishes, raw, small, without tops.														
4 radishes	40	5	Trace	Trace	---	---	1	12	.4	Trace	.01	.01	.1	10
Sauerkraut, canned, solids and liquid.														
1 cup	235	45	2	Trace	---	---	9	85	1.2	120	.07	.09	.4	33
Spinach:														
Cooked														
1 cup	180	40	5	1	---	---	6	167	4.0	14,580	.13	.25	1.0	50
Canned, drained solids														
1 cup	180	45	5	1	---	---	6	212	4.7	14,400	.03	.21	.6	24

Food, Approximate Measure, and Weight (in Grams)	Food Energy	Protein	Fat (Total Lipid)	Fatty acids			Carbohydrate	Calcium	Iron	Vitamin A Value	Thiamine	Riboflavin	Niacin	Ascorbic Acid
				Saturated (Total)	Unsaturated Oleic	Linoleic								
	(Calories)	(Gm.)	(Gm.)	(Gm.)	(Gm.)	(Gm.)	(Gm.)	(Mo.)	(Mo.)	(I.U.)	(Mo.)	(Mo.)	(Mo.)	(Mo.)
	Grams													
Canned, strained or chopped (baby food). 1 ounce	28	10	1	Trace	——	——	——	2	18	.2	1,420	.01	.04	.1	2
Sprouts, raw:														
Mung bean 1 cup	90	30	3	Trace	——	——	——	6	17	1.2	20	.12	.12	.7	17
Soybean 1 cup	107	40	6	2	——	——	——	4	46	.7	90	.17	.16	.8	4
Squash:														
Cooked:														
Summer, diced 1 cup	210	30	2	Trace	——	——	——	7	52	.8	820	.10	.16	1.6	21
Winter, baked, mashed. 1 cup	205	130	4	1	——	——	——	32	57	1.6	8,610	.10	.27	1.4	27
Canned, winter, strained and chopped (baby food). 1 ounce	28	10	Trace	Trace	——	——	——	2	7	.1	510	.01	.01	.1	1
Sweetpotatoes:														
Cooked, medium, 5 by 2 inches, weight raw about 6 ounces:														
Baked, peeled after baking. 1 sweetpotato	110	155	2	1	——	——	——	36	44	1.0	8,910	0.10	0.07	0.7	24
Boiled, peeled after boiling. 1 sweetpotato	147	170	2	1	——	——	——	39	47	1.0	11,610	.13	.09	.9	25
Candied, 3½ by 2¼ inches. 1 sweetpotato	175	295	2	6	2	3	1	60	65	1.6	11,030	.10	.08	.8	17
Canned, vacuum or solid pack. 1 cup	218	235	4	Trace	——	——	——	54	54	1.7	17,000	.10	.10	1.4	30

Food	Grams	Calories	Protein	Fat			Carbohydrate	Calcium	Iron	Vitamin A	Thiamine	Riboflavin	Niacin	Ascorbic acid
Tomatoes:														
Raw, medium, 2 by 2½ inches, about 3 per pound.														
1 tomato	150	35	2	Trace	---	---	7	20	.8	1,350	.10	.06	1.0	34[6]
Canned														
1 cup	242	50	2	Trace	---	---	10	15	1.2	2,180	.13	.07	1.7	40
Tomato juice, canned														
1 cup	242	45	2	Trace	---	---	10	17	2.2	1,940	.13	.07	1.8	39
Tomato catsup														
1 tablespoon	17	15	Trace	Trace	---	---	4	4	.1	240	.02	.01	.3	3
Turnips, cooked, diced														
1 cup	155	35	1	Trace	---	---	8	54	.6	Trace	.06	.08	.5	33
Turnip greens:														
Cooked:														
In small amount of water, short time.														
1 cup	145	30	3	Trace	---	---	5	267	1.6	9,140	.21	.36	.8	100
In large amount of water, long time.														
1 cup	145	25	3	Trace	---	---	5	252	1.4	8,260	.14	.33	.8	68
Canned, solids and liquid														
1 cup	232	40	3	1	---	---	7	232	3.7	10,900	.04	.21	1.4	44
FRUITS AND FRUIT PRODUCTS														
Apples, raw, medium, 2½-inch diameter, about 3 per pound.[4]														
1 apple	150	70	Trace	Trace	---	---	18	8	.4	50	.04	.02	.1	3
Apple brown betty														
1 cup	230	345	4	8	4	Trace	68	41	1.4	230	.13	.10	.9	3
Apple juice, bottled or canned.														
1 cup	249	120	Trace	Trace	---	---	30	15	1.5	---	.01	.04	.2	2
Applesauce, canned:														
Sweetened														
1 cup	254	230	1	Trace	---	---	60	10	1.3	100	.05	.03	.1	3
Unsweetened or artificially sweetened.														
1 cup	239	100	Trace	Trace	---	---	26	10	1.2	100	.04	.02	.1	2

[6]Year-round average. Samples marketed from November through May average around 15 milligrams per 150-gram tomato; from June through October, around 39 milligrams.

Food, Approximate Measure, and Weight (in Grams)	Grams	Food Energy	Protein	Fat (Total Lipid)	Fatty acids Saturated (Total)	Unsaturated Oleic	Unsaturated Linoleic	Carbohydrate	Calcium	Iron	Vitamin A Value	Thiamine	Riboflavin	Niacin	Ascorbic Acid
	Grams	(Calories)	(Gm.)	(Gm.)	(Gm.)	(Gm.)	(Gm.)	(Gm.)	(Mg.)	(Mg.)	(I.U.)	(Mg.)	(Mg.)	(Mg.)	(Mg.)
Applesauce and apricots, canned, strained or junior (baby food). 1 ounce	28	25	Trace	Trace	—	—	—	6	1	.1	170	Trace	Trace	Trace	1
Apricots:															
Raw, about 12 per pound.[4] 3 apricots	114	55	1	Trace	—	—	—	14	18	.5	2,890	.03	.04	.7	10
Canned in heavy sirup: Halves and sirup 1 cup	259	220	2	Trace	—	—	—	57	28	.8	4,510	.05	.06	.9	10
Halves (medium) and sirup, 4 halves; 2 tablespoons sirup	122	105	1	Trace	—	—	—	27	13	.4	2,120	.02	.03	.4	5
Dried: Uncooked, 40 halves, small. 1 cup	150	390	8	1	—	—	—	100	100	8.2	16,350	.02	.23	4.9	19
Cooked, unsweetened, fruit and liquid. 1 cup	285	240	5	1	—	—	—	62	63	5.1	8,550	.01	.13	2.8	8
Apricot nectar, canned 1 cup	250	140	1	Trace	—	—	—	36	22	.5	2,380	.02	.02	.5	7
Avocados, raw: California varieties, mainly Fuerte: 10-ounce avocado, about 3⅓ by 4¼ inches, peeled, pitted. ½ avocado	108	185	2	18	4	8	2	6	11	.6	310	.12	.21	1.7	15
½-inch cubes 1 cup	152	260	3	26	5	12	3	9	15	.9	440	.16	.30	2.4	21

[4]Measure and weight apply to entire vegetable or fruit including parts not usually eaten.

Food and measure	Grams	Food energy (cal.)	Protein (g)	Fat (g)	Saturated (g)	Oleic (g)	Linoleic (g)	Carbohydrate (g)	Calcium (mg)	Iron (mg)	Vitamin A (I.U.)	Thiamine (mg)	Riboflavin (mg)	Niacin (mg)	Ascorbic acid (mg)
Florida varieties: 13-ounce avocado, about 4 by 3 inches, peeled, pitted. ½ avocado	123	160	2	14	3	6	2	11	12	.7	360	.13	.24	2.0	17
½-inch cubes 1 cup	152	195	2	17	3	8	2	13	15	.9	440	.16	.30	2.4	21
Bananas, raw, 6 by 1½ inches, about 3 per pound.[4] 1 banana	150	85	1	Trace	——	——	——	23	8	.7	190	.05	.06	.7	10
Blackberries, raw 1 cup	144	85	2	1	——	——	——	19	46	1.3	290	.05	.06	.5	30
Blueberries, raw 1 cup	140	85	1	1	——	——	——	21	21	1.4	140	.04	.08	.6	20
Cantaloups, raw; medium, 5-inch diameter, about 1⅔ pounds.[4] ½ melon	385	60	1	Trace	——	——	——	14	27	.8	6,540[7]	.08	.06	1.2	63
FRUITS AND FRUIT PRODUCTS—Con. Cherries: Raw, sweet, with stems[4] 1 cup	130	80	2	Trace	——	——	——	20	26	0.5	130	0.06	0.07	0.5	12
Canned, red, sour, pitted, heavy sirup. 1 cup	260	230	2	1	——	——	——	59	36	.8	1,680	.07	.06	.4	13
Cranberry juice cocktail, canned. 1 cup	250	160	Trace	Trace	——	——	——	41	12	.8	Trace	.02	.02	.1	[8]
Cranberry sauce, sweetened, canned, strained. 1 cup	277	405	Trace	1	——	——	——	104	17	.6	40	.03	.03	.1	5
Dates, domestic, natural and dry, pitted, cut. 1 cup	178	490	4	1	——	——	——	130	105	5.3	90	.16	.17	3.9	0
Figs: Raw, small, 1½-inch diameter, about 12 per pound. 3 figs	114	90	1	Trace	——	——	——	23	40	.7	90	.07	.06	.5	2

[7] Value based on varieties with orange-colored flesh; for green-fleshed varieties value is about 540 I.U. per ½ melon.

[8] About 5 milligrams per 8 fluid ounces from cranberries. Ascorbic acid is usually added to approximately 100 milligrams per 8 fluid ounces.

Food, Approximate Measure, and Weight (in Grams)		Food Energy	Pro- tein	Fat (Total Lipid)	Fatty acids			Carbo- hy- drate	Cal- cium	Iron	Vita- min A Value	Thia- mine	Ribo- flavin	Niacin	Ascor- bic Acid
					Satu- rated (Total)	Unsaturated									
						Oleic	Linoleic								
	Grams	(Calo- ries)	(Gm.)	(Gm.)	(Gm.)	(Gm.)	(Gm.)	(Gm.)	(Mo.)	(Mo.)	(I.U.)	(Mo.)	(Mo.)	(Mo.)	(Mo.)
Dried, large, 2 by 1 inch — 1 fig	21	60	1	Trace	-----	-----	-----	15	26	.6	20	.02	.02	.1	0
Fruit cocktail, canned in heavy sirup, solids and liquid — 1 cup	256	195	1	1	-----	-----	-----	50	23	1.0	360	.04	.03	1.1	5
Grapefruit: Raw, medium, 4¼-inch diameter, size 64: White⁴ — ½ grapefruit	285	55	1	Trace	-----	-----	-----	14	22	.6	10	.05	.02	.3	52
Pink or red⁴ — ½ grapefruit	285	60	1	Trace	-----	-----	-----	15	23	.6	640	.05	.02	.3	52
Raw sections, white — 1 cup	194	75	1	Trace	-----	-----	-----	20	31	.8	20	.07	.03	.3	72
Canned, white: Sirup pack, solids and liquid. — 1 cup	249	175	1	Trace	-----	-----	-----	44	32	.7	20	.07	.04	.5	75
Water pack, solids and liquid. — 1 cup	240	70	1	Trace	-----	-----	-----	18	31	.7	20	.07	.04	.5	72
Grapefruit juice: Fresh — 1 cup	246	95	1	Trace	-----	-----	-----	23	22	.5	(9)	.09	.04	.4	92
Canned, white: Unsweetened — 1 cup	247	100	1	Trace	-----	-----	-----	24	20	1.0	20	.07	.04	.4	84
Sweetened — 1 cup	250	130	1	Trace	-----	-----	-----	32	20	1.0	20	.07	.04	.4	78

⁹For white-fleshed varieties value is about 20 I.U. per cup; for red-fleshed varieties, 1,080 I.U. per cup.

Food	Measure	g	cal	protein g	fat g		carb g	mg	mg	I.U.	mg	mg	mg	mg
Frozen, concentrate, unsweetened: Undiluted, can, 6 fluid ounces.	1 can	207	300	4	1	----	72.	70	.8	60	.29	.12	1.4	286
Diluted with 3 parts water, by volume.	1 cup	247	100	1	Trace	----	24	25	.2	20	.10	.04	.5	96
Frozen, concentrate, sweetened: Undiluted, can, 6 fluid ounces.	1 can	211	350	3	1	----	85	59	.6	50	.24	.11	1.2	245
Diluted with 3 parts water, by volume.	1 cup	249	115	1	Trace	----	28	20	.2	20	.08	.03	.4	82
Dehydrated: Crystals, net weight 4 ounces.	1 can	114	430	5	1	----	103	99	1.1	90	.41	.18	2.0	399
Prepared with water (1 pound yields about 1 gallon).	1 cup	247	100	1	Trace	----	24	22	.2	20	.10	.05	.5	92
Grapes, raw: American type (slip skin), such as Concord, Delaware, Niagara, Catawba, and Scuppernong[4]	1 cup	153	65	1	1	----	15	15	.4	100	.05	.03	.2	3
European type (adherent skin), such as Malaga, Muscat, Thompson Seedless, Emperor, and Flame Tokay.[4]	1 cup	160	95	1	Trace	----	25	17	.6	140	.07	.04	.4	6
Grape juice, bottled or canned.	1 cup	254	165	1	Trace	----	42	28	.8	----	.10	.05	.6	Trace
Lemons, raw, medium, 2⅛-inch diameter, size 150.[4]	1 lemon	106	20	1	Trace	----	6	18	.4	10	.03	.01	.1	38

[4]Measure and weight apply to entire vegetable or fruit including parts not usually eaten.

129

Food, Approximate Measure, and Weight (In Grams)	Grams	Food Energy (Calories)	Protein (Gm.)	Fat (Total Lipid) (Gm.)	Fatty acids Saturated (Total) (Gm.)	Unsaturated Oleic (Gm.)	Linoleic (Gm.)	Carbohydrate (Gm.)	Calcium (Mg.)	Iron (Mg.)	Vitamin A Value (I.U.)	Thiamine (Mg.)	Riboflavin (Mg.)	Niacin (Mg.)	Ascorbic Acid (Mg.)
Lemon juice:															
Fresh 1 cup	246	60	1	Trace				20	17	.5	40	.08	.03	.2	113
1 tablespoon	15	5	Trace	Trace				1	1	Trace	Trace	Trace	Trace	Trace	7
Canned, unsweetened 1 cup	245	55	1	Trace				19	17	.5	40	.07	.03	.2	102
Lemonade concentrate, frozen, sweetened:															
Undiluted, can, 6 fluid ounces. 1 can	220	430	Trace	Trace				112	9	.4	40	.05	.06	.7	66
Diluted with 4½ parts water, by volume. 1 cup	248	110	Trace	Trace				28	2	.1	10	.01	.01	.2	17
Lime juice:															
Fresh 1 cup	246	65	1	Trace				22	22	0.5	30	0.05	0.03	0.3	80
Canned 1 cup	246	65	1	Trace				22	22	.5	30	.05	.03	.3	52
Limeade concentrate, frozen, sweetened:															
Undiluted, can, 6 fluid ounces. 1 can	218	410	Trace	Trace				108	11	.2	Trace	.02	.02	.2	26
Diluted with 4⅓ parts water, by volume. 1 cup	248	105	Trace	Trace				27	2	Trace	Trace	Trace	Trace	Trace	6
Oranges, raw: California, Navel (winter), 2-4/5-inch diameter, size 88.[4]															

Food, approximate measure	Weight (grams)	Food energy (Calories)	Protein (grams)	Fat, total (grams)	Saturated (grams)	Oleic (grams)	Linoleic (grams)	Carbohydrate (grams)	Calcium (mg)	Iron (mg)	Vitamin A (I.U.)	Thiamine (mg)	Riboflavin (mg)	Niacin (mg)	Ascorbic acid (mg)
1 orange	180	60	2	Trace	—	—	—	16	49	.5	240	.12	.05	.5	75
Florida, all varieties, 3-inch diameter.[4] 1 orange	210	75	1	Trace	—	—	—	19	67	.3	310	.16	.06	.6	70
Orange juice: Fresh: California, Valencia (summer). 1 cup	249	115	2	1	—	—	—	26	27	.7	500	.22	.06	.9	122
Florida varieties: Early and midseason. 1 cup	247	100	1	Trace	—	—	—	23	25	.5	490	.22	.06	.9	127
Late season, Valencia. 1 cup	248	110	1	Trace	—	—	—	26	25	.5	500	.22	.06	.9	92
Canned, unsweetened 1 cup	249	120	2	Trace	—	—	—	28	25	1.0	500	.17	.05	.6	100
Frozen concentrate: Undiluted, can, 6 fluid ounces. 1 can	210	330	5	Trace	—	—	—	80	69	.8	1,490	.63	.10	2.4	332
Diluted with 3 parts water, by volume. 1 cup	248	110	2	Trace	—	—	—	27	22	.2	500	.21	.03	.8	112
Dehydrated: Crystals, can, net weight 4 ounces. 1 can	113	430	6	2	—	—	—	100	95	1.9	1,900	.76	.24	3.3	406
Prepared with water, 1 pound yields about 1 gallon. 1 cup	248	115	1	Trace	—	—	—	27	25	.5	500	.20	.06	.9	108
Orange and grapefruit juice: Frozen concentrate: Undiluted, can, 6 fluid ounces. 1 can	209	325	4	1	—	—	—	78	61	.8	790	.47	.06	2.3	301
Diluted with 3 parts water, by volume. 1 cup	248	110	1	Trace	—	—	—	26	20	.2	270	.16	.02	.8	102
Papayas, raw, ½-inch cubes. 1 cup	182	70	1	Trace	—	—	—	18	36	.5	3,190	.07	.08	.5	102

[4] Measure and weight apply to entire vegetable or fruit including parts not usually eaten.

Food, Approximate Measure, and Weight (in Grams)		Food Energy	Pro-tein	Fat (Total Lipid)	Fatty acids			Carbo-hy-drate	Cal-cium	Iron	Vita-min A Value	Thia-mine	Ribo-flavin	Niacin	Ascor-bic Acid
					Satu-rated (Total)	Unsaturated Oleic	Unsaturated Linoleic								
	Grams	(Calo-ries)	(Gm.)	(Gm.)	(Gm.)	(Gm.)	(Gm.)	(Gm.)	(Mo.)	(Mo.)	(I.U.)	(Mo.)	(Mo.)	(Mo.)	(Mo.)
Peaches:															
Raw:															
Whole, medium, 2-inch diameter about 4 per pound.[a]															
1 peach	114	35	1	Trace	----	----	----	10	9	.5	[101]1,320	.02	.05	1.0	7
Sliced															
1 cup	168	65	1	Trace	----	----	----	16	15	.8	[102]2,230	.03	.08	1.6	12
Canned, yellow-fleshed, solids and liquid:															
Sirup pack, heavy:															
Halves or slices															
1 cup	257	200	1	Trace	----	----	----	52	10	.8	1,100	.02	.06	1.4	7
Halves (medium) and sirup.															
2 halves and 2 tablespoons sirup	117	90	Trace	Trace	----	----	----	24	5	.4	500	.01	.03	.7	3
Water pack															
1 cup	245	75	1	Trace	----	----	----	20	10	.7	1,000	.02	.06	1.4	7
Strained or chopped (baby food).															
1 ounce	28	25	Trace	Trace	----	----	----	6	2	.1	140	Trace	.01	.2	1
Dried:															
Uncooked															
1 cup	160	420	5	1	----	----	----	109	77	9.6	6,240	.02	.31	8.5	28
Cooked, unsweetened, 10-12 halves and 6 tablespoons liquid.															

[101][102]Based on yellow-fleshed varieties; for white-fleshed varieties value is about 50 I.U. per 114-gram peach and 80 I.U. per cup of sliced peaches.

Food, approximate measure	Grams	Food energy (calories)	Protein (g)	Fat (g)		Carbohydrate (g)	Calcium (mg)	Iron (mg)	Vitamin A (I.U.)	Thiamine (mg)	Riboflavin (mg)	Niacin (mg)	Ascorbic acid (mg)
1 cup	270	220	3	1	—	58	41	5.1	3,290	.01	.15	4.2	6
Frozen:													
Carton, 12 ounces, not thawed. 1 carton	340	300	1	Trace	—	77	14	1.7	2,210	.03	.14	2.4	[11]135
Can, 16 ounces, not thawed. 1 can	454	400	2	Trace	—	103	18	2.3	2,950	.05	.18	3.2	[11]181
Peach nectar, canned 1 cup	250	120	Trace	Trace	—	31	10	.5	1,080	.02	.05	1.0	1
Pears:													
Raw, 3 by 2½-inch diameter.[4] 1 pear	182	100	1	1	—	25	13	.5	30	.04	.07	.2	7
Canned, solids and liquid: Sirup pack, heavy:													
Halves or slices 1 cup	255	195	1	1	—	50	13	0.5	Trace	0.03	0.05	0.3	4
Halves (medium) and sirup. 2 halves and 2 tablespoons sirup	117	90	Trace	Trace	—	23	6	.2	Trace	.01	.02	.2	2
Water pack 1 cup	243	80	Trace	Trace	—	20	12	.5	Trace	.02	.05	.3	4
Strained or chopped (baby food). 1 ounce	28	20	Trace	Trace	—	5	2	.1	10	Trace	.01	.1	1
Pear nectar, canned 1 cup	250	130	1	Trace	—	33	8	.2	Trace	.01	.05	Trace	1
Persimmons, Japanese or kaki, raw, seedless, 2½-inch diameter.[4] 1 persimmon	125	75	1	Trace	—	20	6	.4	2,740	.03	.02	.1	11
Pineapple:													
Raw, diced 1 cup	140	75	1	Trace	—	19	24	.7	100	.12	.04	.3	24
Canned, heavy sirup pack, solids and liquid: Crushed 1 cup	260	195	1	Trace	—	50	29	.8	120	.20	.06	.5	17

[11]Average weighed in accordance with commercial freezing practices. For products without added ascorbic acid, value is about 37 milligrams per 12-ounce carton and 50 milligrams per 16-ounce can; for those with added ascorbic acid, 139 milligrams per 12 ounces and 186 milligrams per 16 ounces.

[4]Measure and weight apply to entire vegetable or fruit including parts not usually eaten.

Food, Approximate Measure, and Weight (in Grams)	Grams	Food Energy (Calories)	Protein (Gm.)	Fat (Total Lipid) (Gm.)	Fatty acids Saturated (Total) (Gm.)	Unsaturated Oleic (Gm.)	Linoleic (Gm.)	Carbohydrate (Gm.)	Calcium (Mg.)	Iron (Mg.)	Vitamin A Value (I.U.)	Thiamine (Mg.)	Riboflavin (Mg.)	Niacin (Mg.)	Ascorbic Acid (Mg.)
Sliced, slices and juice. 2 small or 1 large and 2 tablespoons juice	122	90	Trace	Trace	---	---	---	24	13	.4	50	.09	.03	.2	8
Pineapple juice, canned 1 cup	249	135	1	Trace	---	---	---	34	37	.7	120	.12	.04	.5	22
Plums, all except prunes: Raw, 2-inch diameter, about 2 ounces.[4] 1 plum	60	25	Trace	Trace	---	---	---	7	7	.3	140	.02	.02	.3	3
Canned, sirup pack (Italian prunes): Plums (with pits) and juice.[4] 1 cup	256	205	1	Trace	---	---	---	53	22	2.2	2,970	.05	.05	.9	4
Plums (without pits) and juice. 3 plums and 2 tablespoons juice	122	100	Trace	Trace	---	---	---	26	11	1.1	1,470	.03	.02	.5	2
Prunes, dried, "softenized", medium: Uncooked[4] 4 prunes	32	70	1	Trace	---	---	---	18	14	1.1	440	.02	.04	.4	1
Cooked, unsweetened, 17-18 prunes and 1/3 cup liquid.[4] 1 cup	270	295	2	1	---	---	---	78	60	4.5	1,860	.08	.18	1.7	2
Prunes with tapioca, canned, strained or junior (baby food). 1 ounce	28	25	Trace	Trace	---	---	---	6	2	.3	110	.01	.02	.1	1
Prune juice, canned 1 cup	256	200	1	Trace	---	---	---	49	36	10.5	---	.02	.03	1.1	4
Raisins, dried 1 cup	160	460	4	Trace	---	---	---	124	99	5.6	30	.18	.13	.9	2

Raspberries, red:

Food	Measure	Grams	Food energy	Protein	Fat	Saturated	Oleic	Linoleic	Carbohydrate	Calcium	Iron	Vitamin A	Thiamine	Riboflavin	Niacin	Ascorbic acid
Raw	1 cup	123	70	1	1	—	—	—	17	27	1.1	160	.04	.11	1.1	31
Frozen, 10-ounce carton, not thawed	1 carton	284	275	2	1	—	—	—	70	37	1.7	200	.06	.17	1.7	59
Rhubarb, cooked, sugar added	1 cup	272	385	1	Trace	—	—	—	98	212	1.6	220	.06	.15	.7	17
Strawberries: Raw, capped	1 cup	149	55	1	1	—	—	—	13	31	1.5	90	.04	.10	1.0	88
Frozen, 10-ounce carton, not thawed	1 carton	284	310	1	1	—	—	—	79	40	2.0	90	.06	.17	1.5	150
Frozen, 16-ounce can, not thawed	1 can	454	495	2	1	—	—	—	126	64	3.2	150	.09	.27	2.4	240
Tangerines, raw, medium, 2½-inch diameter, about 4 per pound.[4]	1 tangerine	114	40	1	Trace	—	—	—	10	34	.3	350	.05	.02	.1	26
Tangerine juice: Canned, unsweetened	1 cup	248	105	1	Trace	—	—	—	25	45	.5	1,040	.14	.04	.3	56
Frozen concentrate: Undiluted, can, 6 fluid ounces.	1 can	210	340	4	1	—	—	—	80	130	1.5	3,070	.43	.12	.9	202
Diluted, with 3 parts water, by volume.	1 cup	248	115	1	Trace	—	—	—	27	45	.5	1,020	.14	.04	.3	67
Watermelon, raw, wedge, 4 by 8 inches (1/16 of 10 by 16-inch melon, about 2 pounds with rind).[4]	1 wedge	925	115	2	1	—	—	—	27	30	2.1	2,510	.13	.13	.7	30

GRAIN PRODUCTS

Food	Measure	Grams	Food energy	Protein	Fat	Saturated	Oleic	Linoleic	Carbohydrate	Calcium	Iron	Vitamin A	Thiamine	Riboflavin	Niacin	Ascorbic acid
Barley, pearled, light, uncooked.	1 cup	203	710	17	2	Trace	1	—	160	32	4.1	0	0.25	0.17	6.3	0
Biscuits, baking powder with enriched flour, 2½-inch diameter.	1 biscuit	38	140	3	6	2	3	1	17	46	.6	Trace	.08	.08	.7	Trace

[4]Measure and weight apply to entire vegetable or fruit including parts not usually eaten.

Food, Approximate Measure, and Weight (in Grams)	Food Energy	Protein	Fat (Total Lipid)	Fatty acids Saturated (Total)	Fatty acids Unsaturated Oleic	Fatty acids Unsaturated Linoleic	Carbohydrate	Calcium	Iron	Vitamin A Value	Thiamine	Riboflavin	Niacin	Ascorbic Acid
Grams	(Calories)	(Gm.)	(Gm.)	(Gm.)	(Gm.)	(Gm.)	(Gm.)	(Mg.)	(Mg.)	(I.U.)	(Mg.)	(Mg.)	(Mg.)	(Mg.)
Bran flakes (40 percent bran) added thiamine.														
1 ounce	28	85	3	1	—	—	—	23	20	1.2	0	.11	.05	1.7	0
Breads:														
Boston brown bread, slice, 3 by ¾ inch.														
1 slice	48	100	3	1	—	—	—	22	43	.9	0	.05	.03	.6	0
Cracked-wheat bread:														
Loaf, 1-pound, 20 slices.														
1 loaf	454	1190	39	10	2	5	2	236	399	5.0	Trace	.53	.42	5.8	Trace
Slice														
1 slice	23	60	2	1	—	—	—	12	20	.3	Trace	.03	.02	.3	Trace
French or Vienna bread:														
Enriched, 1-pound loaf.														
1 loaf	454	1315	41	14	3	8	2	251	195	10.0	Trace	1.26	.98	11.3	Trace
Unenriched, 1-pound loaf.														
1 loaf	454	1315	41	14	3	8	2	251	195	3.2	Trace	.39	.39	3.6	Trace
Italian bread:														
Enriched, 1-pound loaf.														
1 loaf	454	1250	41	4	Trace	1	2	256	77	10.0	0	1.31	.93	11.7	0
Unenriched, 1-pound loaf.														
1 loaf	454	1250	41	4	Trace	1	2	256	77	3.2	0	.39	.27	3.6	0
Raisin bread:														
Loaf, 1-pound, 20 slices.														
1 loaf	454	1190	30	13	3	8	2	243	322	5.9	Trace	.24	.42	3.0	Trace
Slice														
1 slice	23	60	2	1	—	—	—	12	16	.3	Trace	.01	.02	.2	Trace
Rye bread:														

Food															
American, light (⅓ rye, ⅔ wheat):															
Loaf, 1-pound, 20 slices.															
1 loaf	454	1100	41	5	—	—	—	236	340	7.3	0	.81	.33	6.4	0
Slice	23	55	2	Trace	—	—	—	12	17	.4	0	.04	.02	.3	0
Pumpernickel, loaf, 1 pound.															
1 loaf	454	1115	41	5	—	—	—	241	381	10.9	0	1.05	.63	5.4	0
White bread, enriched:															
1 to 2 percent nonfat dry milk:															
Loaf, 1-pound, 20 slices.															
1 loaf	454	1225	39	15	3	8	2	229	318	10.9	Trace	1.13	.77	10.4	Trace
Slice	23	60	2	1	Trace	Trace	Trace	12	16	.6	Trace	.06	.04	.5	Trace
3 to 4 percent nonfat dry milk:[12]															
Loaf, 1-pound															
1 loaf	454	1225	39	15	3	8	2	229	381	11.3	Trace	1.13	.95	10.8	Trace
Slice, 20 per loaf															
1 slice	23	60	2	1	Trace	Trace	Trace	12	19	.6	Trace	.06	.05	.6	Trace
Slice, toasted															
1 slice	20	60	2	1	Trace	Trace	Trace	12	19	.6	Trace	.05	.05	.6	Trace
Slice, 26 per loaf															
1 slice	17	45	1	1	Trace	Trace	Trace	9	14	.4	Trace	.04	.04	.4	Trace
5 to 6 percent nonfat dry milk:															
Loaf, 1-pound, 20 slices.															
1 loaf	454	1245	41	17	4	10	2	228	435	11.3	Trace	1.22	.91	11.0	Trace
Slice	23	65	2	1	Trace	Trace	Trace	12	22	.6	Trace	.06	.05	.6	Trace
White bread, unenriched:															
1 to 2 percent nonfat dry milk:															
Loaf, 1-pound, 20 slices.															
1 loaf	454	1225	39	15	3	8	2	229	318	3.2	Trace	.40	.36	5.6	Trace
Slice	23	60	2	1	Trace	Trace	Trace	12	16	.2	Trace	.02	.02	.3	Trace
3 to 4 percent nonfat dry milk:[12]															
Loaf, 1-pound															
1 loaf	454	1225	39	15	3	8	2	229	318	3.2	Trace	.40	.36	5.6	Trace
1 slice	23	60	2	1	Trace	Trace	Trace	12	16	.2	Trace	.02	.02	.3	Trace

[12]When the amount of nonfat dry milk in commercial white bread is unknown, values for bread with 3 to 4 percent nonfat dry milk are suggested.

| Food, Approximate Measure, and Weight (in Grams) | Food Energy | Protein | Fat (Total Lipid) | Fatty acids | | | Carbohydrate | Calcium | Iron | Vitamin A Value | Thiamine | Riboflavin | Niacin | Ascorbic Acid |
| | | | | Saturated (Total) | Unsaturated Oleic | Linoleic | | | | | | | | |
	(Calories)	(Gm.)	(Gm.)	(Gm.)	(Gm.)	(Gm.)	(Gm.)	(Mg.)	(Mg.)	(I.U.)	(Mg.)	(Mg.)	(Mg.)	(Mg.)
	Grams													
1 loaf	454 1225	39	15	3	8	3	229	381	3.2	Trace	.31	.39	5.0	Trace
Slice, 20 per loaf 1 slice	23 60	2	1	Trace	Trace	Trace	12	19	.2	Trace	.02	.02	.3	Trace
Slice, toasted 1 slice	20 60	2	1	Trace	Trace	Trace	12	19	.2	Trace	.01	.02	.3	Trace
Slice, 26 per loaf 1 slice	17 45	1	1	Trace	Trace	Trace	9	14	.1	Trace	.01	.01	.2	Trace
5 to 6 percent nonfat dry milk:														
Loaf, 1 pound, 20 slices. 1 loaf	454 1245	41	17	4	10	2	228	435	3.2	Trace	.32	.59	4.1	Trace
Slice 1 slice	23 65	2	1	Trace	Trace	Trace	12	22	.2	Trace	.02	.03	.2	Trace
Whole-wheat bread, made with 2 percent nonfat dry milk:														
Loaf, 1-pound, 20 slices 1 loaf	454 1105	48	14	3	6	3	216	449	10.4	Trace	1.17	.56	12.9	Trace
Slice 1 slice	23 55	2	1	Trace	Trace	Trace	11	23	.5	Trace	.06	.03	.7	Trace
Slice, toasted 1 slice	19 55	2	1	Trace	Trace	Trace	11	22	.5	Trace	.05	.03	.6	Trace
Breadcrumbs, dry, grated 1 cup	88 345	11	4	1	2	1	65	107	3.2	Trace	.19	.26	3.1	Trace
Cakes:[18]														
Angelfood cake; sector, 2-inch (1/12 of 8-inch-diameter cake). 1 sector	40 110	3	Trace				24	4	.1	0	Trace	.06	.1	0

[18] Unenriched cake flour and vegetable cooking fat used unless otherwise specified.

Cakes[13]—Continued

Food	Weight (g)														
Chocolate cake, chocolate icing; sector, 2-inch (1/16 of 10-inch-diameter layer cake). 1 sector	120	445	5	20	8	10	1	67	84	1.2	190[14]	0.03	0.12	0.3	Trace
Fruitcake, dark (made with enriched flour); piece, 2 by 2 by ½ inch. 1 piece	30	115	1	5	1	3	1	18	22	.8	40[14]	.04	.04	.2	Trace
Gingerbread (made with enriched flour); piece, 2 by 2 by 2 inches. 1 piece	55	175	2	6	1	4	Trace	29	37	1.3	50	.06	.06	.5	0
Plain cake and cupcakes, without icing: Piece, 3 by 2 by 1½ inches. 1 piece	55	200	2	8	2	5	1	31	35	.2	90[14]	.01	.05	.1	Trace
Cupcake, 2¾-inch diameter. 1 cupcake	40	145	2	6	1	3	Trace	22	26	.2	70[14]	.01	.03	.1	Trace
Plain cake and cupcakes, with chocolate icing; Sector, 2 inch (1/16 of 10-inch-layer cake). 1 sector	100	370	4	14	5	7	1	59	63	.6	180[14]	.02	.09	.2	Trace
Cupcake, 2¾-inch diameter. 1 cupcake	50	185	2	7	2	4	Trace	30	32	.3	90[14]	.01	.04	.1	Trace
Poundcake, oldfashioned (equal weights flour, sugar, fat, eggs); slice, 2¾ by 3 by ⅝ inch. 1 slice	30	140	2	9	2	5	1	14	6	.2	80[14]	.01	.03	.1	0
Sponge cake; sector, 2-inch (1/12 of 8-inch-diameter cake). 1 sector	40	120	3	2	1	1	Trace	22	12	.5	180	.02	.06	.1	Trace

[13]Unenriched cake flour and vegetable cooking fat used unless otherwise specified.

[14]If the fat used in the recipe is butter or fortified margarine, the vitamin A value for chocolate cake with chocolate icing will be 490 I.U. per 2-inch, 100 I.U. for fruitcake, 300 I.U. for plain cake without icing, 220 I.U. per piece, 220 I.U. per cupcake, for plain cake with icing, 440 I.U. per 2-inch sector, 220 I.U. per cupcake, and 300 I.U. for poundcake.

Food, Approximate Measure, and Weight (In Grams)	Grams	Food Energy (Calories)	Protein (Gm.)	Fat (Total Lipid) (Gm.)	Fatty acids Saturated (Total) (Gm.)	Unsaturated Oleic (Gm.)	Linoleic (Gm.)	Carbohydrate (Gm.)	Calcium (Mg.)	Iron (Mg.)	Vitamin A Value (I.U.)	Thiamine (Mg.)	Riboflavin (Mg.)	Niacin (Mg.)	Ascorbic Acid (Mg.)
Cookies:															
Plain and assorted, 3-inch diameter.															
1 cooky	25	120	1	5	—	—	—	18	9	.2	20	.01	.01	.1	Trace
Fig bars, small															
1 fig bar	16	55	1	1	—	—	—	12	12	.2	20	.01	.01	.1	Trace
Corn, rice and wheat flakes, mixed, added nutrients.															
1 ounce	28	110	2	Trace	—	—	—	24	11	.5	0	.11	—	.9	0
Corn flakes, added nutrients:															
Plain															
1 ounce	28	110	2	Trace	—	—	—	24	5	.4	0	.12	.02	.6	0
Sugar-covered															
1 ounce	28	110	1	Trace	—	—	—	26	3	.3	0	.12	.01	.5	0
Corn grits, degermed, cooked:															
Enriched															
1 cup	242	120	3	Trace	—	—	—	27	2	[15].7	0	[15].10	[15].07	[15]1.0	0
Unenriched															
1 cup	242	120	3	Trace	—	—	—	27	2	.2	0	.05	.02	.5	0
Cornmeal, white or yellow, dry:															
Whole ground, unbolted															
1 cup	118	420	11	5	1	2	2	87	24	2.8	[16]600	.45	.13	2.4	0
Degermed, enriched															
1 cup	145	525	11	2	Trace	1	1	114	9	[15]4.2	[16]640	[15].64	[15].38	[15]5.1	0

[15] Iron, thiamine, riboflavin, and niacin are based on the minimum levels of enrichment specified in standards of identity promulgated under the Federal Food, Drug, and Cosmetic Act.

Food	Grams	Calories								Vit. A				
Corn muffins, made with enriched degermed cornmeal and enriched flour; muffin, 2¾-inch diameter. 1 muffin	48	150	3	5	2	Trace	23	50	.8	[17]80	.09	.11	.8	Trace
Corn, puffed, presweetened, added nutrients. 1 ounce	28	110	1	Trace	---	---	26	3	.5	0	.12	.05	.6	0
Corn, shredded, added nutrients. 1 ounce	28	110	2	Trace	---	---	25	1	.7	0	.12	.05	.6	0
Crackers:														
Graham, plain. 4 small or 2 medium	14	55	1	1	---	---	10	6	.2	0	.01	.03	.2	0
Saltines, 2 inches square. 2 crackers	8	35	1	1	---	---	6	2	.1	0	Trace	Trace	.1	0
Soda:														
Cracker, 2½ inches square. 2 crackers	11	50	1	1	Trace	Trace	8	2	.2	0	Trace	Trace	.1	0
Oyster crackers. 10 crackers	10	45	1	1	Trace	Trace	7	2	.2	0	Trace	Trace	.1	0
Cracker meal. 1 tablespoon	10	45	1	1	Trace	Trace	7	2	.1	0	.01	Trace	.1	0
Doughnuts, cake type. 1 doughnut	32	125	1	6	1	4	16	13	[18].4	30	[18].05	[18].05	[18].4	Trace
Farina, regular, enriched, cooked. 1 cup	238	100	3	Trace	---	---	21	10	[15].7	0	[15].11	[15].07	[15]1.0	0

141

[16]Vitamin A value based on yellow product. White product contains only a trace.

[17]Based on recipe using white cornmeal; if yellow cornmeal is used, the vitamin A value is 140 I.U. per muffin.

[18]Based on product made with enriched flour. With unenriched flour, approximate values per doughnut are: Iron, 0.2 milligram; thiamine, 0.2 milligram; riboflavin, 0.03 milligram; niacin, 0.2 milligram.

Food, Approximate Measure, and Weight (in Grams)	Grams	Food Energy (Calories)	Protein (Gm.)	Fat (Total Lipid) (Gm.)	Fatty acids Saturated (Total) (Gm.)	Unsaturated Oleic (Gm.)	Unsaturated Linoleic (Gm.)	Carbohydrate (Gm.)	Calcium (Mg.)	Iron (Mg.)	Vitamin A Value (I.U.)	Thiamine (Mg.)	Riboflavin (Mg.)	Niacin (Mg.)	Ascorbic Acid (Mg.)
Macaroni, cooked: Enriched: Cooked, firm stage (8 to 10 minutes; undergoes additional cooking in a food mixture).															
1 cup	130	190	6	1	—	—	—	39	14	[15]1.4	0	[15]0.23	[15]0.14	[15]1.9	0
Cooked until tender															
1 cup	140	155	5	1	—	—	—	32	11	[15]1.3	0	[15].19	[15].11	[15]1.5	0
Unenriched: Cooked, firm stage (8 to 10 minutes; undergoes additional cooking in a food mixture).															
1 cup	130	190	6	1	—	—	—	39	14	.6	0	.02	.02	.5	0
Cooked until tender															
1 cup	140	155	5	1	—	—	—	32	11	.6	0	.02	.02	.4	0
Macaroni (enriched) and cheese, baked.															
1 cup	220	470	18	24	11	10	1	44	398	2.0	950	.22	.44	2.0	Trace
Muffins, with enriched white flour; muffin, 2¾-inch diameter.															
1 muffin	48	140	4	5	1	3	Trace	20	50	.8	50	.08	.11	.7	Trace
Noodles (egg noodles), cooked: Enriched															
1 cup	160	200	7	2	1	1	Trace	37	16	[15]1.4	110	[15].23	[15].14	[15]1.8	0
Unenriched															
1 cup	160	200	7	2	1	1	Trace	37	16	1.0	110	.04	.03	.7	0

[15] Iron, thiamine, riboflavin, and niacin are based on the minimum levels of enrichment specified in standards of identity promulgated under the Federal Food, Drug, and Cosmetic Act.

Food															
Oats (with or without corn) puffed, added nutrients. 1 ounce	28	115	3	2	Trace	1	1	21	50	1.3	0	.28	.05	.5	0
Oatmeal or rolled oats, regular or quick-cooking, cooked. 1 cup	236	130	5	2	Trace	1	1	23	21	1.4	0	.19	.05	.3	0
Pancakes (griddlecakes), 4-inch diameter: Wheat, enriched flour (home recipe). 1 cake	27	60	2	2	Trace	1	Trace	9	27	.4	30	.05	.06	.3	Trace
Buckwheat (buckwheat pancake mix, made with egg and milk). 1 cake	27	55	2	2	1	1	Trace	6	59	.4	60	.03	.04	.2	Trace
Piecrust, plain, baked: Enriched flour: Lower crust, 9-inch shell. 1 crust	135	675	8	45	10	20	3	59	19	2.3	0	.27	.19	2.4	0
Double crust, 9-inch pie. 1 double crust	270	1350	16	90	21	58	7	118	38	4.6	0	.55	.39	4.9	0
Unenriched flour: Lower crust, 9-inch shell. 1 crust	135	675	8	45	10	29	3	59	19	.7	0	.04	.04	.6	0
Double crust, 9-inch pie. 1 double crust	270	1350	16	90	21	58	7	118	38	1.4	0	.08	.07	1.3	0
Pies (piecrust made with unenriched flour); sector, 4-inch, 1/7 of 9-inch-diameter pie. Apple. 1 sector	135	345	3	15	4	9	1	51	11	.4	40	.03	.02	.5	1
Cherry. 1 sector	135	355	4	15	4	10	1	52	19	.4	590	.03	.03	.6	1
Custard. 1 sector	130	280	8	14	5	8	1	30	125	.8	300	.07	.21	.4	0
Lemon meringue. 1 sector	120	305	4	12	4	7	1	45	17	.6	200	.04	.10	.2	4
Mince. 1 sector	135	365	3	16	4	10	1	56	38	1.4	Trace	.09	.05	.5	1
Pumpkin. 1 sector	130	275	5	15	5	7	1	32	66	.6	3,210	.04	.13	.6	Trace

Food, Approximate Measure, and Weight (in Grams)		Food Energy	Pro-tein	Fat (Total Lipid)	Fatty acids			Carbo-hy-drate	Cal-cium	Iron	Vita-min A Value	Thia-mine	Ribo-flavin	Niacin	Ascor-bic Acid
					Satu-rated (Total)	Unsaturated									
						Oleic	Linoleic								
	Grams	(Calories)	(Gm.)	(Gm.)	(Gm.)	(Gm.)	(Gm.)	(Gm.)	(Mg.)	(Mg.)	(I.U.)	(Mg.)	(Mg.)	(Mg.)	(Mg.)
Pizza (cheese); 5½-inch sector; 1/8 of 14-inch-diameter pie. 1 sector	75	185	7	6	2	3	Trace	27	107	.7	290	.04	.12	.7	4
Popcorn, popped, with added oil and salt. 1 cup	14	65	1	3	2	Trace	Trace	8	1	.3	—	—	.01	.2	0
Pretzels, small stick 5 sticks	5	20	Trace	Trace	—	—	—	4	1	0	0	Trace	Trace	Trace	0
Rice, white (fully milled or polished), enriched, cooked; Common commercial varieties, all types. 1 cup	168	185	3	Trace	—	—	—	41	17	[20]1.5	0	[20].19	[20].01	[20]1.6	0
Long grain, parboiled 1 cup	176	185	4	Trace	—	—	—	41	33	[20]1.4	0	[20].19	[20].02	[20]2.0	0
Rice, puffed, added nutrients (without salt). 1 cup	14	55	1	Trace	—	—	—	13	3	.3	0	.06	.01	.6	0
Rice flakes, added nutrients. 1 cup	30	115	2	Trace	—	—	—	26	9	0.5	0	0.10	0.02	1.6	0
Rolls: Plain, pan; 12 per 16 ounces: Enriched															

[20]Iron, thiamine, and niacin are based on the minimum levels of enrichment specified in standards of identity promulgated under the Federal Food, Drug, and Cosmetic Act. Riboflavin is based on unenriched rice. When the minimum level of enrichment for riboflavin specified in the standards of identity becomes effective the value will be 0.12 milligram per cup of parboiled rice and of white rice.

Food	Grams	Cal.	Protein	Fat	Sat.	Oleic	Lino.	Carb.	Calcium	Iron	Vit. A	Thiamin	Ribo.	Niacin	Vit. C
1 roll	38	115	3	2	Trace	1	Trace	20	28	.7	Trace	.11	.07	.8	Trace
Unenriched 1 roll	38	115	3	2	Trace	1	Trace	20	28	.3	Trace	.02	.03	.3	Trace
Hard, round; 12 per 22 ounces. 1 roll	52	160	5	2	Trace	1	Trace	31	24	.4	Trace	.03	.05	.4	Trace
Sweet, pan; 12 per 18 ounces. 1 roll	43	135	4	4	1	2	Trace	21	37	.3	30	.03	.06	.4	Trace
Rye wafers, whole-grain, 1⅞ by 3½ inches. 2 wafers	13	45	2	Trace	—	—	—	10	7	.5	0	.04	.03	.2	0
Spaghetti:															
Cooked, tender stage (14 to 20 minutes):															
Enriched 1 cup	140	155	5	1	—	—	1	32	11	[16]1.3	0	[15].19	[15].11	[16]1.5	0
Unenriched 1 cup	140	155	5	1	—	—	1	32	11	.6	0	.02	.02	.4	0
Spaghetti with meat balls in tomato sauce (home recipe), 1 cup	250	335	19	12	4	6	1	39	125	3.8	1,600	.26	.30	4.0	22
Spaghetti in tomato sauce with cheese (home recipe), 1 cup	250	260	9	9	2	5	1	37	80	2.2	1,080	.24	.18	2.4	14
Waffles, with enriched flour, ½ by 4½ by 5½ inches. 1 waffle	75	210	7	7	2	4	1	28	85	1.3	250	.13	.19	1.0	Trace
Wheat, puffed:															
With added nutrients (without salt). 1 ounce	28	105	4	Trace	—	—	—	22	8	1.2	0	.15	.07	2.2	0
With added nutrients, with sugar and honey. 1 ounce	28	105	2	1	—	—	—	25	7	.9	0	.14	.05	1.8	0
Wheat, rolled; cooked 1 cup	236	175	5	1	—	—	—	40	19	1.7	0	.17	.06	2.1	0
Wheat, shredded, plain (long, round, or bitesize). 1 ounce	28	100	3	1	—	—	—	23	12	1.0	0	.06	.03	1.2	0

Food, Approximate Measure, and Weight (in Grams)	Grams	Food Energy (Calories)	Protein (Gm.)	Fat (Total Lipid) (Gm.)	Fatty acids Saturated (Total) (Gm.)	Unsaturated Oleic (Gm.)	Unsaturated Linoleic (Gm.)	Carbohydrate (Gm.)	Calcium (Mo.)	Iron (Mo.)	Vitamin A Value (I.U.)	Thiamine (Mo.)	Riboflavin (Mo.)	Niacin (Mo.)	Ascorbic Acid (Mo.)
Wheat and malted barley flakes, with added nutrients. 1 ounce	28	110	2	Trace	---	---	---	24	14	.7	0	.13	.03	1.1	0
Wheat flakes, with added nutrients. 1 ounce	28	100	3	Trace	---	---	---	23	12	1.2	0	.18	.04	1.4	0
Wheat flours: Whole-wheat, from hard wheats, stirred. 1 cup	120	400	16	2	Trace	1	1	85	49	4.0	0	.66	.14	5.2	0
All-purpose or family flour: Enriched, sifted 1 cup	110	400	12	1	Trace	Trace	Trace	84	18	[15]3.2	0	[15].48	[15].29	[15]3.8	0
Unenriched, sifted 1 cup	110	400	12	1	Trace	Trace	Trace	84	18	.9	0	.07	.05	1.0	0
Self-rising, enriched 1 cup	110	385	10	1	Trace	Trace	Trace	82	292	[15]3.2	0	[15].49	[15].29	[15]3.9	0
Cake or pastry flour, sifted. 1 cup	100	365	8	1	Trace	Trace	Trace	79	17	.5	0	.03	.03	.7	0
Wheat germ, crude, commercially milled. 1 cup	68	245	18	7	1	2	4	32	49	6.4	0	1.36	.46	2.9	0
FATS, OILS															
Butter, 4 sticks per pound: Sticks, 2 1 cup	277	1625	1	184	101	61	6	1	45	0	[30]7,500	---	---	---	0

13Iron, thiamine, riboflavin, and niacin are based on the minimum levels of enrichment specified in standards of identity promulgated under the Federal Food, Drug, and Cosmetic Act.

146

Food and measure	Grams	Food energy		Fat	Saturated	Oleic	Linoleic	Carbo-hydrate	Calcium	Iron	Vitamin A	Thiamine	Riboflavin	Niacin	Ascorbic acid
Sticks, 1/8															
1 tablespoon	14	100	Trace	11	6	4	Trace	Trace	3	0	[20]460	—	—	—	0
Pat or square (64 per pound). 1 pat	7	50	Trace	6	3	2	Trace	Trace	1	0	[20]230	—	—	—	0
Fats, cooking:															
Lard															
1 cup	200	1985	0	220	84	101	22	0	0	0	0	0	0	0	0
1 tablespoon	14	125	0	14	5	6	1	0	0	0	0	0	0	0	0
Vegetable fats															
1 cup	200	1770	0	200	46	130	14	0	0	0	0	0	0	0	0
1 tablespoon	12.5	110	0	12	3	8	1	0	0	—	0	—	—	—	0
Margarine, 4 sticks per pound:															
Sticks, 2															
1 cup	227	1635	1	184	37	105	33	1	45	0	[21]17,500	0	0	0	0
Stick, 1/8															
1 tablespoon	14	100	Trace	11	2	6	2	Trace	3	0	[21]460	—	—	—	0
Pat or square (64 per pound). 1 pat	7	50	Trace	6	1	3	1	Trace	1	0	[21]230	—	—	—	0
Oils, salad or cooking:															
Corn															
1 tablespoon	14	125	0	14	1	4	7	0	0	0	0	0	0	0	0
Cottonseed															
1 tablespoon	14	125	0	14	4	3	7	0	0	0	0	0	0	0	0
Olive															
1 tablespoon	14	125	0	14	2	11	1	0	0	0	0	0	0	0	0
Soybean															
1 tablespoon	14	125	0	14	2	3	7	0	0	0	0	0	0	0	0
Salad dressings:															
Blue cheese															
1 tablespoon	16	80	1	8	2	2	4	1	13	Trace	30	Trace	0.02	Trace	Trace
Commercial, mayonnaise type. 1 tablespoon	15	65	Trace	6	1	1	3	2	2	Trace	30	Trace	Trace	Trace	Trace

[20]Year-round average.

[21]Based on the average vitamin A content of fortified margarine. Federal specifications for fortified margarine require a minimum of 15,000 I.U. of vitamin A per pound.

Food, Approximate Measure, and Weight (in Grams)	Grams	Food Energy (Calories)	Protein (Gm.)	Fat (Total Lipid) (Gm.)	Fatty acids Saturated (Total) (Gm.)	Unsaturated Oleic (Gm.)	Linoleic (Gm.)	Carbohydrate (Gm.)	Calcium (Mg.)	Iron (Mg.)	Vitamin A Value (I.U.)	Thiamine (Mg.)	Riboflavin (Mg.)	Niacin (Mg.)	Ascorbic Acid (Mg.)
French 1 tablespoon	15	60	Trace	6	1	1	3	3	2	.1	---	---	---	---	---
Home cooked, boiled 1 tablespoon	17	30	1	2	1	1	Trace	3	15	.1	80	.01	.03	Trace	Trace
Mayonnaise 1 tablespoon	15	110	Trace	12	2	3	6	Trace	3	.1	40	Trace	.01	Trace	---
Thousand Island 1 tablespoon	15	75	Trace	8	1	2	4	2	2	.1	50	Trace	Trace	Trace	Trace

SUGARS, SWEETS

Food, Approximate Measure, and Weight (in Grams)	Grams	Food Energy (Calories)	Protein (Gm.)	Fat (Total Lipid) (Gm.)	Fatty acids Saturated (Total) (Gm.)	Unsaturated Oleic (Gm.)	Linoleic (Gm.)	Carbohydrate (Gm.)	Calcium (Mg.)	Iron (Mg.)	Vitamin A Value (I.U.)	Thiamine (Mg.)	Riboflavin (Mg.)	Niacin (Mg.)	Ascorbic Acid (Mg.)
Candy:															
Caramels 1 ounce	28	115	1	3	2	1	Trace	22	42	.4	Trace	.01	.05	Trace	Trace
Chocolate, milk, plain 1 ounce	28	150	2	9	5	3	Trace	16	65	.3	80	.02	.09	.1	Trace
Fudge, plain 1 ounce	28	115	1	3	2	1	Trace	21	22	.3	Trace	.01	.03	.1	Trace
Hard candy 1 ounce	28	110	0	Trace	---	---	---	28	6	.5	0	0	0	0	0
Marshmallows 1 ounce	28	90	1	Trace	---	---	---	23	5	.5	0	0	Trace	Trace	0
Chocolate sirup, thin type 1 tablespoon	20	50	Trace	Trace	Trace	Trace	---	13	3	.3	---	Trace	.01	.1	0
Honey, strained or extracted, 1 tablespoon	21	65	Trace	0	---	---	---	17	1	.1	0	Trace	.01	.1	Trace
Jams and preserves 1 tablespoon	20	55	Trace	Trace	---	---	---	14	4	.2	Trace	Trace	.01	Trace	Trace
Jellies 1 tablespoon	20	55	Trace	Trace	---	---	---	14	4	.3	Trace	Trace	.01	Trace	1

Molasses, cane:

Light (first extraction) 1 tablespoon	20	50	---	---	---	13	33	.9	---	.01	.01	Trace	---
Blackstrap (third extraction) 1 tablespoon	20	45	---	---	---	11	137	3.2	---	.02	.04	.4	---
Sirup, table blends (chiefly corn, light and dark) 1 tablespoon	20	60	0	0	0	15	9	.8	0	0	0	0	0
Sugars (cane or beet):													
Granulated 1 cup	200	770	0	0	0	199	0	.2	0	0	0	0	0
1 tablespoon	12	45	0	0	0	12	0	Trace	0	0	0	0	0
Lump, 1⅛ by ¾ by ⅜ 1 lump	6	25	0	0	0	6	0	Trace	0	0	0	0	0
Powdered, stirred before measuring. 1 cup	128	495	0	0	0	127	0	.1	0	0	0	0	0
1 tablespoon	8	30	0	0	0	8	0	Trace	0	0	0	0	0
Brown, firm-packed 1 cup	220	820	0	0	0	212	187	7.5	0	.02	.07	.4	0
1 tablespoon	14	50	0	0	0	13	12	.5	0	Trace	Trace	Trace	0

MISCELLANEOUS ITEMS

Beer (average 3.6 percent alcohol by weight). 1 cup	240	100	1	0	---	9	12	Trace	---	.01	.07	1.6	---
Beverages, carbonated:													
Cola type 1 cup	240	95	0	0	---	24	---	---	0	0	0	0	0
Ginger ale 1 cup	230	70	0	0	---	18	---	---	0	0	0	0	0
Bouillon cube, ⅝ inch 1 cube	4	5	1	Trace	Trace	Trace	---	---	---	---	---	---	---
Chili powder, See Vegetables, peppers.													
Chili sauce (mainly tomatoes). 1 tablespoon	17	20	Trace	Trace	---	4	3	.1	240	.02	.01	.3	3
Chocolate:													
Bitter or baking 1 ounce	28	145	3	15	8	6	Trace	22	1.9	20	.01	.07	.4	0

149

Food, Approximate Measure, and Weight (in Grams)	Food Energy	Protein	Fat (Total Lipid)	Fatty acids Saturated (Total)	Unsaturated Oleic	Linoleic	Carbohydrate	Calcium	Iron	Vitamin A Value	Thiamine	Riboflavin	Niacin	Ascorbic Acid
	(Calories)	(Gm.)	(Gm.)	(Gm.)	(Gm.)	(Gm.)	(Gm.)	(Mo.)	(Mo.)	(I.U.)	(Mo.)	(Mo.)	(Mo.)	(Mo.)
Sweet — 1 ounce — Grams 28	150	1	10	6	4	Trace	16	27	.4	Trace	.01	.04	.1	Trace
Cider. See Fruits, apple juice.														
Gelatin, dry:														
Plain — 1 tablespoon — 10	35	9	Trace	---	---	---	---	---	---	---	---	---	---	---
Desert powder, 3-ounce package. — 85	315	8	0	---	---	---	75	---	---	---	---	---	---	---
Gelatin dessert, ready-to-eat:														
Plain — 1 cup — 239	140	4	0	---	---	---	34	---	---	---	---	---	---	---
With fruit — 1 cup — 241	160	3	Trace	---	---	---	40	---	---	---	---	---	---	---
Olives, pickled:														
Green — 4 medium or 3 extra large or 2 giant — 16	15	Trace	2	Trace	2	Trace	Trace	8	.2	40	---	---	---	---
Ripe: Mission — 3 small or 2 large — 10	15	Trace	2	Trace	2	Trace	Trace	9	.1	10	Trace	Trace	---	---
Pickles, cucumber:														
Dill, large, 4 by 1¾ inches. — 1 pickle — 135	15	1	Trace	---	---	---	3	35	1.4	140	Trace	.03	Trace	8
Sweet, 2¾ by ¾ inches — 1 pickle — 20	30	Trace	Trace	---	---	---	7	2	.2	20	Trace	Trace	Trace	1
Popcorn. See Grain products.														
Sherbet, orange. — 1 cup — 193	260	2	2	---	---	---	59	31	Trace	110	.02	.06	Trace	4
Soups, canned; ready-to-serve (prepared														

with equal volume of water):

Food	Measure														
Bean with pork	1 cup	250	170	8	6	1	2	2	22	62	2.2	650	.14	.07	1.0	2
Beef noodle	1 cup	250	70	4	3	1	1	1	7	8	1.0	50	.05	.06	1.1	Trace
Beef bouillon, broth, consomme	1 cup	240	30	5	0	0	0	0	3	Trace	.5	Trace	Trace	.02	1.2	---
Chicken noodle	1 cup	250	65	4	2	Trace	1	1	8	10	0.5	50	0.02	0.02	0.8	Trace
Clam chowder	1 cup	255	85	2	2		3	5	13	36	1.0	920	.03	.03	1.0	---
Cream soup (mushroom)	1 cup	240	135	2	10	1			10	41	.5	70	.02	.12	.7	Trace
Minestrone	1 cup	245	105	5	3		2	1	14	37	1.0	2,350	.07	.05	1.0	7
Pea, green	1 cup	245	130	6	2	1		Trace	23	44	1.0	340	.05	.05	1.0	7
Tomato	1 cup	245	90	2	2	Trace	2	1	16	15	.7	1,000	.05	.05	1.1	12
Vegetable with beef broth	1 cup	250	80	3	2				14	20	.8	3,250	.05	.02	1.2	---
Starch (cornstarch)	1 cup	128	465	Trace	Trace				112	0	0	0	0	0	0	0
	1 tablespoon	8	30	Trace	Trace				7	0	0	0	0	0	0	0
Tapioca, quick-cooking granulated, dry, stirred before measuring.	1 cup	152	535	1	Trace				131	15	.6	0	0	0	.6	0
	1 tablespoon	10	35	Trace	Trace				9	1	Trace	0	0	0	Trace	0
Vinegar	1 tablespoon	15	2	0	0				1	1	.1	---	---	---	---	---
White sauce, medium	1 cup	265	430	10	33	18	11	1	23	305	.5	1,220	.12	.44	.6	Trace
Yeast: Baker's: Compressed	1 ounce	28	25	3	Trace	Trace			3	4	1.4	Trace	.20	.47	3.2	Trace
Dry active	1 ounce	28	80	10	Trace	Trace			11	12	4.6	Trace	.66	1.53	10.4	Trace

Food, Approximate Measure, and Weight (in Grams)		Food Energy	Pro- tein	Fat (Total Lipid)	Fatty acids			Carbo- hy- drate	Cal- cium	Iron	Vita- min A Value	Thia- mine	Ribo- flavin	Niacin	Ascor- bic Acid
					Satu- rated (Total)	Unsaturated									
						Oleic	Linoleic								
	Grams	(Calo- ries)	(Gm.)	(Gm.)	(Gm.)	(Gm.)	(Gm.)	(Gm.)	(Mo.)	(Mo.)	(I.U.)	(Mo.)	(Mo.)	(Mo.)	(Mo.)
Brewer's, dry, debittered. 1 tablespoon ------	8	25	3	Trace	----	----	----	3	17	1.4	Trace	1.25	.34	3.0	Trace
Yoghurt. See Milk, cream, cheese; related products.															

AMINO ACID CONTENT OF FOODS, 100 GM., EDIBLE PORTION

Protein Content, and Nitrogen Conversion Factor	Tryptophan (Gm.)	Threonine (Gm.)	Iso-leucine (Gm.)	Leucine (Gm.)	Lysine (Gm.)	Methionine (Gm.)	Cystine (Gm.)	Phenylalanine (Gm.)	Tyrosine (Gm.)	Valine (Gm.)	Arginine (Gm.)	Histidine (Gm.)
Milk; Milk Products												
Milk (Ptn, N×6.38):												
cow:												
fluid, whole and non-fat (3.5% ptn)	0.049	0.161	0.223	0.344	0.272	0.086	0.031	0.170	0.178	0.240	0.128	0.092
canned:												
evaporated, unsweetened (7.0% ptn)	0.099	0.323	0.447	0.688	0.545	0.171	0.063	0.340	0.357	0.481	0.256	0.185
condensed, sweetened (8.1% ptn)	0.114	0.374	0.518	0.796	0.631	0.198	0.072	0.393	0.413	0.557	0.296	0.214
dried:												
whole (25.8% ptn)	0.364	1.191	1.648	2.535	2.009	0.632	0.231	1.251	1.316	1.774	0.944	0.680
non-fat (35.6% ptn)	0.502	1.641	2.271	3.493	2.768	0.870	0.318	1.724	1.814	2.444	1.300	0.937
human (1.4% ptn)	0.023	0.062	0.075	0.278	0.312	0.065	0.027	0.121	0.071	0.139	0.174	0.068
goat (3.3% ptn)	0.039	0.217	0.087	0.124	0.090	0.028	0.058	0.060	—	0.086	0.055	0.030
Indian buffalo (4.2% ptn)	0.059	0.212	0.204	0.420	0.331	0.112	0.058	0.177	—	0.255	0.136	0.086
Milk products:												
buttermilk (3.5% ptn, N×6.38)	0.038	0.165	0.219	0.348	0.291	0.082	0.032	0.186	0.137	0.262	0.168	0.099
casein (100.0% ptn, N×6.29)	1.335	4.277	6.550	13.048	8.013	3.084	0.382	5.389	5.819	7.393	4.070	3.021
cheese (ptn, N×6.38):												
blue mold (21.5% ptn)	0.293	0.799	1.449	2.096	1.577	0.559	0.121	1.153	1.028	1.543	0.785	0.701
Camembert (17.5% ptn)	0.239	0.650	1.179	1.706	1.284	0.455	0.099	0.938	0.837	1.256	0.639	0.571
Cheddar (25.0% ptn)	0.341	0.929	1.685	2.437	1.834	0.650	0.141	1.340	1.195	1.794	0.913	0.815
Cheddar processed (23.2% ptn)	0.316	0.862	1.563	2.262	1.702	0.604	0.131	1.244	1.109	1.665	0.847	0.756
cheese foods, Cheddar (20.5% ptn)	0.280	0.761	1.382	1.998	1.504	0.533	0.116	1.099	0.980	1.472	0.749	0.668
cottage (17.0% ptn)	0.179	0.794	0.989	1.826	1.428	0.469	0.147	0.917	0.917	0.978	0.802	0.549
cream cheese (9.0% ptn)	0.080	0.408	0.519	0.923	0.721	0.229	0.085	0.547	0.408	0.538	0.313	0.278
Limburger (21.2% ptn)	0.289	0.788	1.429	2.067	1.555	0.552	0.120	1.136	1.014	1.522	0.774	0.691
Parmesan (36.0% ptn)	0.491	1.337	2.426	3.510	2.641	0.937	0.203	1.930	1.721	2.584	1.315	1.174
Swiss (27.5% ptn)	0.375	1.021	1.853	2.574	1.937	0.687	0.149	1.415	1.262	1.895	0.964	0.861
Swiss processed (26.4% ptn)	0.360	0.981	1.779									
lactalbumin (100.0% ptn, N×6.49)	2.203	5.239	6.209	12.342	9.060	2.250	3.405	4.360	3.806	5.686	3.498	1.911
whey (Ptn, N×6.49):												
fluid (0.9% ptn)	0.010	0.048	0.052	0.074	0.055	0.013	0.018	0.023	0.009	0.045	0.017	0.011
dried (12.7% ptn)	0.147	0.677	0.734	1.043	0.769	0.188	0.250	0.323	0.131	0.640	0.235	0.159

Protein Content, and Nitrogen Conversion Factor	Trypto-phan (Gm.)	Threo-nine (Gm.)	Iso-leucine (Gm.)	Leucine (Gm.)	Lysine (Gm.)	Methi-onine (Gm.)	Cystine (Gm.)	Phenyl-alanine (Gm.)	Tyro-sine (Gm.)	Valine (Gm.)	Argi-nine (Gm.)	Histi-dine (Gm.)
EGGS, CHICKEN (Ptn, N×6.25)												
Fresh or stored:												
whole (12.8% ptn)	0.211	0.637	0.850	1.126	0.819	0.401	0.299	0.739	0.551	0.950	0.840	0.307
whites (10.8% ptn)	0.164	0.477	0.698	0.950	0.648	0.420	0.263	0.689	0.449	0.842	0.634	0.233
yolks (16.3% ptn)	0.235	0.827	0.996	1.372	1.074	0.417	0.274	0.717	0.756	1.121	1.132	0.368
Dried:												
whole (46.8% ptn)	0.771	2.329	3.108	4.118	2.995	1.468	1.093	2.703	2.014	3.474	3.070	1.123
whites (85.9% ptn)	1.306	3.793	5.553	7.559	5.154	3.340	2.089	5.484	3.573	6.693	5.044	1.855
yolks (31.2% ptn)	0.449	1.582	1.907	2.626	2.057	0.799	0.524	1.373	1.448	2.147	2.167	0.704
MEAT; POULTRY, FISH AND SHELLFISH; THEIR PRODUCTS												
Meat (Ptn, N×6.25):												
beef carcass or side:												
thin (18.8% ptn)	0.220	0.830	0.984	1.540	1.642	0.466	0.238	0.773	0.638	1.044	1.212	0.653
medium fat (17.5% ptn)	0.204	0.773	0.916	1.434	1.529	0.434	0.221	0.720	0.594	0.972	1.128	0.608
fat (16.3% ptn)	0.190	0.720	0.853	1.335	1.424	0.404	0.206	0.670	0.553	0.905	1.051	0.566
very fat (13.7% ptn)	0.160	0.605	0.717	1.122	1.197	0.340	0.173	0.563	0.465	0.761	0.883	0.476
medium fat, trimmed to retail basis (18.2% ptn)	0.213	0.804	0.952	1.491	1.590	0.451	0.230	0.748	0.617	1.010	1.174	0.632
beef cuts, medium fat:												
chuck (18.6% ptn)	0.217	0.821	0.973	1.524	1.625	0.461	0.235	0.765	0.631	1.033	1.199	0.646
flank (19.9% ptn)	0.232	0.879	1.041	1.630	1.738	0.494	0.252	0.818	0.675	1.105	1.283	0.691
hamburger (16.0% ptn)	0.187	0.707	0.837	1.311	1.398	0.397	0.207	0.658	0.543	0.888	1.032	0.556
porterhouse (16.4% ptn)	0.192	0.724	0.858	1.343	1.433	0.407	0.220	0.674	0.556	0.911	1.057	0.569
rib roast (17.4% ptn)	0.203	0.768	0.910	1.425	1.520	0.432	0.220	0.715	0.590	0.966	1.122	0.604
round (19.5% ptn)	0.228	0.861	1.020	1.597	1.704	0.484	0.246	0.802	0.661	1.083	1.257	0.677
rump (16.2% ptn)	0.189	0.715	0.848	1.327	1.415	0.402	0.205	0.666	0.550	0.899	1.045	0.562
sirloin (17.3% ptn)	0.202	0.764	0.905	1.417	1.511	0.429	0.219	0.711	0.587	0.960	1.116	0.601
beef, canned (25.0% ptn)	0.292	1.104	1.308	2.048	2.184	0.620	0.316	1.028	0.848	1.388	1.612	0.868
beef, dried or chipped (34.3% ptn)	0.401	1.515	1.795	2.810	2.996	0.851	0.434	1.410	1.163	1.904	2.212	1.191
lamb carcass or side:												
thin (17.1% ptn)	0.222	0.782	0.886	1.324	1.384	0.410	0.224	0.695	0.594	0.843	1.114	0.476
medium fat (15.7% ptn)	0.203	0.718	0.814	1.216	1.271	0.377	0.206	0.638	0.545	0.774	1.022	0.437
fat (13.0% ptn)	0.168	0.595	0.674	1.007	1.052	0.312	0.171	0.528	0.451	0.641	0.847	0.362

lamb cuts, medium fat:												
leg (18.0% ptn)	0.233	0.824	0.933	1.394	1.457	0.432	0.236	0.732	0.625	0.887	1.172	0.501
rib (14.9% ptn)	0.193	0.682	0.772	1.154	1.206	0.358	0.195	0.606	0.517	0.734	0.970	0.415
shoulder (15.6% ptn)	0.202	0.714	0.809	1.208	1.263	0.374	0.205	0.634	0.542	0.769	1.016	0.434
pork, packer's carcass or side:												
thin (14.1% ptn)	0.183	0.654	0.724	1.038	1.157	0.352	0.165	0.555	0.503	0.733	0.864	0.487
medium fat (11.9% ptn)	0.154	0.552	0.611	0.876	0.977	0.297	0.139	0.468	0.425	0.619	0.729	0.411
fat (9.8% ptn)	0.127	0.455	0.503	0.721	0.804	0.245	0.114	0.386	0.330	0.510	0.601	0.339
pork cuts, medium fat, fresh:												
ham (15.2% ptn)	0.197	0.705	0.781	1.119	1.248	0.379	0.178	0.598	0.542	0.790	0.931	0.525
loin (16.4% ptn)	0.213	0.761	0.842	1.207	1.346	0.409	0.192	0.646	0.585	0.853	1.005	0.567
miscellaneous lean cuts (14.5% ptn)	0.188	0.673	0.745	1.067	1.190	0.362	0.169	0.571	0.517	0.754	0.889	0.501
pork, cured:												
bacon, medium fat (9.1% ptn)	0.095	0.306	0.399	0.728	0.587	0.141	0.106	0.434	0.234	0.434	0.622	0.246
fat back or salt pork (3.9% ptn)	0.006	0.141	0.110	0.367	0.317	0.055	0.043	0.157	0.052	0.168	0.379	0.035
ham (16.9% ptn)	0.162	0.692	0.841	1.306	1.420	0.411	0.273	0.646	0.652	0.879	1.068	0.544
luncheon meat:												
boiled ham (22.8% ptn)	0.219	0.934	1.135	1.762	1.915	0.554	0.368	0.872	0.879	1.186	1.441	0.733
canned, spiced (14.9% ptn)	0.143	0.610	0.741	1.151	1.252	0.362	0.241	0.570	0.575	0.775	0.942	0.479
rabbit, domesticated, flesh only (21.0% ptn)	——	1.021	1.082	1.636	1.818	0.541	——	0.793	——	1.021	1.176	0.474
veal, carcass or side:												
thin (19.7% ptn)	0.258	0.854	1.040	1.444	1.645	0.451	0.233	0.801	0.709	1.018	1.283	0.634
medium fat (19.1% ptn)	0.251	0.828	1.008	1.400	1.595	0.437	0.226	0.776	0.688	0.987	1.244	0.614
fat (18.5% ptn)	0.243	0.802	0.977	1.356	1.545	0.423	0.219	0.752	0.666	0.956	1.205	0.595
veal cuts, medium fat:												
round (19.5% ptn)	0.256	0.846	1.030	1.429	1.629	0.446	0.231	0.792	0.702	1.008	1.270	0.627
shoulder (19.4% ptn)	0.255	0.841	1.024	1.422	1.620	0.444	0.230	0.788	0.698	1.003	1.263	0.624
stew meat (18.3% ptn)	0.240	0.793	0.966	1.341	1.528	0.419	0.217	0.744	0.659	0.946	1.192	0.589
Poultry (Ptn, N×6.25):												
chicken, flesh only:												
broilers or fryers (20.6% ptn)	0.250	0.877	1.088	1.490	1.810	0.537	0.277	0.811	0.725	1.012	1.302	0.593
hens (21.3% ptn)	0.259	0.907	1.125	1.540	1.871	0.556	0.286	0.838	0.750	1.046	1.346	0.613
ducks, domesticated, flesh only (21.4% ptn)	——	0.935	1.109	1.657	1.842	0.531	——	0.842	——	1.027	1.301	0.486
turkey, flesh only (24.0% ptn)	——	1.014	1.260	1.836	2.173	0.664	0.330	0.960	——	1.187	1.513	0.649

MEAT; POULTRY; FISH—Continued

Protein Content, and Nitrogen Conversion Factor (Ptn, N×6.25):	Trypto-phan (Gm.)	Threo-nine (Gm.)	Iso-leucine (Gm.)	Leucine (Gm.)	Lysine (Gm.)	Methi-onine (Gm.)	Cystine (Gm.)	Phenyl-alanine (Gm.)	Tyro-sine (Gm.)	Valine (Gm.)	Argi-nine (Gm.)	Histi-dine (Gm.)
Products from meat, poultry, and fish (Ptn, N×6.25):												
brains (10.4% ptn)	0.138	0.494	0.504	0.845	0.760	0.220	0.145	0.506	0.433	0.536	0.614	0.278
chitterlings (8.6% ptn)	0.094	0.398	0.308	0.457	0.670	0.193	0.109	0.359	0.228	0.462	1.406	0.169
fish flour (76.0% ptn)	0.754	4.378	4.232	6.189	7.381	2.019		2.845		3.916	5.204	1.289
gelatin (85.6% ptn, N×5.55)	0.006	1.912	1.357	2.930	4.226	0.787	0.077	2.036	0.401	2.421	7.866	0.771
gizzard, chicken (23.1% ptn)	0.207	1.072	1.094	1.689	1.567	0.554	0.218	0.968	0.680	1.116	1.741	0.480
heart:												
beef or pork (16.9% ptn)	0.219	0.776	0.857	1.509	1.387	0.403	0.168	0.765	0.627	0.973	1.068	0.433
chicken (20.5% ptn)	0.266	0.941	1.040	1.830	1.683	0.489	0.203	0.928	0.761	1.181	1.296	0.525
kidney:												
beef (15.0% ptn)	0.221	0.665	0.730	1.301	1.087	0.307	0.182	0.706	0.557	0.876	0.934	0.377
pork (16.3% ptn)	0.240	0.722	0.793	1.414	1.181	0.334	0.198	0.767	0.605	0.952	1.015	0.409
sheep (16.6% ptn)	0.244	0.736	0.807	1.440	1.203	0.340	0.202	0.781	0.616	0.969	1.033	0.417
liver:												
beef or pork (19.7% ptn)	0.296	0.936	1.031	1.819	1.475	0.463	0.243	0.993	0.738	1.239	1.201	0.523
calf (19.0% ptn)	0.286	0.903	0.994	1.754	1.423	0.447	0.234	0.958	0.711	1.195	1.158	0.505
chicken (22.1% ptn)	0.332	1.050	1.156	2.040	1.655	0.520	0.272	1.114	0.827	1.390	1.347	0.587
sheep or lamb (21.0% ptn)	0.316	0.998	1.099	1.939	1.572	0.494	0.259	1.058	0.786	1.320	1.280	0.558
pancreas:												
beef (13.5% ptn)	0.175	0.626	0.683	1.054	0.996	0.244		0.562	0.590	0.724	0.771	0.266
pork (14.5% ptn)	0.188	0.673	0.733	1.132	1.070	0.262		0.603	0.633	0.777	0.828	0.285
pork or beef, canned (14.3% ptn)	0.151	0.618	0.730	1.190	1.345	0.327	0.261	0.579	0.570	0.810	1.050	0.460
potted meat (16.1% ptn)	0.149	0.662	0.641	1.203	1.061	0.361		0.641		0.943	1.002	0.322
sausage:												
Bologna (14.8% ptn)	0.126	0.606	0.718	1.061	1.191	0.313	0.185	0.540	0.481	0.744	1.028	0.308
Braunschweiger (15.4% ptn)	0.172	0.668	0.754	1.291	1.200	0.320	0.187	0.700	0.471	0.956	0.954	0.458
frankfurters (14.2% ptn)	0.120	0.582	0.688	1.018	1.143	0.300	0.177	0.518	0.461	0.713	0.986	0.382
head cheese (15.0% ptn)	0.079	0.418	0.509	0.946	0.907	0.250	0.209	0.569	0.569	0.617	1.075	0.278
liverwurst (16.7% ptn)	0.187	0.724	0.818	1.400	1.301	0.347	0.203	0.759	0.510	1.037	1.034	0.497
pork, links, raw (10.8% ptn)	0.092	0.442	0.524	0.774	0.869	0.228	0.135	0.394	0.351	0.543	0.750	0.290
pork, bulk, canned (15.4% ptn)	0.131	0.631	0.747	1.104	1.239	0.325	0.192	0.562	0.500	0.774	1.069	0.414
salami (23.9% ptn)	0.203	0.979	1.159	1.713	1.923	0.505	0.298	0.872	0.776	1.201	1.660	0.642

MEAT; POULTRY, FISH—Continued

Vienna sausage, canned (15.8% ptn) ---	0.134	0.647	0.766	1.133	1.272	0.334	0.197	0.576	0.513	0.794	1.097	0.425
tongue:												
beef (16.4% ptn) -----	0.197	0.708	0.792	1.286	1.364	0.357	0.207	0.661	0.548	0.840	1.065	0.412
pork (16.8% ptn) -----	0.202	0.726	0.812	1.317	1.398	0.366	0.212	0.677	0.562	0.860	1.091	0.422
veal and pork loaf, canned (17.2% ptn)--	0.198	0.627	0.859	1.236	1.258	0.418	0.209	0.619	0.468	0.958	0.916	0.388

LEGUMES (DRY SEED); COMMON NUTS; OTHER NUTS AND DRY SEEDS; THEIR PRODUCTS.

Legume seeds and their products:												
beans (Phaseolus vulgaris) (N×6.25):												
pinto and red Mexican (23.0% ptn) ---	0.213	0.997	1.306	1.976	1.708	0.232	0.228	1.270	0.887	1.395	1.384	0.655
red kidney:												
raw (23.1% ptn) -----	0.214	1.002	1.312	1.985	1.715	0.233	0.229	1.275	0.891	1.401	1.390	0.658
canned, solids and liquid (5.7% ptn)	0.053	0.247	0.324	0.490	0.423	0.057	0.057	0.315	0.220	0.346	0.343	0.162
other common beans including navy, peabean, white marrow:												
raw (21.4% ptn) -----	0.199	0.928	1.216	1.839	1.589	0.216	0.212	1.181	0.825	1.298	1.287	0.609
baked with pork	0.057	0.274	0.291	0.486	0.354	0.059	0.018	0.333	0.165	0.312	0.251	0.186
black gram, raw (23.6% ptn, N×6.25) --	0.242	0.801	1.390	2.062	1.510	0.332	0.287	1.242	0.551	1.450	1.552	0.559
broadbeans, raw (25.4% ptn, N×6.25) --	0.236	0.829	1.593	2.211	1.426	0.106	0.179	1.057	0.687	1.276	1.780	0.748
chickpeas (20.8% ptn, N÷6.25) -----	0.170	0.739	1.195	1.195	1.434	0.276	0.296	1.012	0.692	1.025	1.551	0.559
cowpeas (22.9% ptn, N×6.25) -----	0.220	0.901	1.110	1.715	1.491	0.352	0.297	1.198	0.678	1.293	1.473	0.692
dolichos, twinflower (21.6% ptn, N×6.25)	0.221	0.836	1.448	1.707	1.700	0.294	0.480	1.486	0.560	1.286	1.230	0.650
lentils, whole (25.0% ptn, N×6.25) --	0.216	0.896	1.316	1.760	1.528	0.180	0.204	1.104	0.664	1.360	1.908	0.548
lima beans (20.7% ptn, N×6.25) ----	0.195	0.980	1.199	1.722	1.378	0.331	0.311	1.222	0.543	1.298	1.315	0.669
lupine (32.3% ptn, N×6.25) -----		1.101	1.618	1.964	1.447	0.114	0.109	1.271	1.245	1.328	2.718	0.811
moth beans (24.4% ptn, N×6.25) ----	0.164	0.765	1.093	1.484	1.202	0.191	0.152	1.003	0.390	0.695	1.370	0.722
mung beans (24.4% ptn, 6.25) -----	0.180	0.828	1.351	2.202	1.667	0.265	0.463	1.167	1.104	1.444		0.543
peanuts (26.9% ptn, N×5.46) -----	0.340		1.266	1.872	1.099	0.271		1.557		1.532	3.296	0.749
peanut flour (51.2% ptn, N×5.46) ----	0.647	1.575	2.410	3.553	2.091	0.516	0.881	2.963	2.100	2.916	6.273	1.425
peanut butter (26.1% ptn, N×5.46) ---	0.330	0.803	1.228	1.816	1.066	0.263	0.449	1.510	1.071	1.487	3.198	0.727
peas (Pisum sativum) (N×6.25):												
entire seeds (23.8% ptn) -----	0.251	0.918	1.340	1.969	1.744	0.286	0.308	1.200	0.960	1.333	2.102	0.651
split (24.5% ptn) ------	0.259	0.945	1.380	2.027	1.795	0.294	0.318	1.235	0.988	1.372	2.164	0.670
pigeonpeas, without seed coat (21.9% ptn, N×6.25) -----	0.119	0.834	1.346	1.717	1.580	0.256	0.308	1.875	0.725	1.153	1.489	0.617

Protein Content, and Nitrogen Conversion Factor	Trypto-phan (Gm.)	Threo-nine (Gm.)	Iso-leucine (Gm.)	Leucine (Gm.)	Lysine (Gm.)	Methi-onine (Gm.)	Cystine (Gm.)	Phenyl-alanine (Gm.)	Tyro-sine (Gm.)	Valine (Gm.)	Argi-nine (Gm.)	Histi-dine (Gm.)
LEGUMES; SEEDS; NUTS—Continued												
soybeans, whole (34.9% ptn, N×5.71)	0.526	1.504	2.054	2.946	2.414	0.513	0.678	1.889	1.216	2.005	2.763	0.911
soybean flour, flakes, and grits (ptn, N×5.71):												
low fat (44.7% ptn)	0.673	1.926	2.630	3.773	3.092	0.658	0.869	2.419	1.558	2.568	3.538	1.166
medium fat (42.5% ptn)	0.640	1.831	2.501	3.588	2.94	0.625	0.826	2.300	1.481	2.441	3.364	1.109
full fat (35.9% ptn)	0.541	1.547	2.112	3.030	2.483	0.528	0.698	1.943	1.251	2.062	2.842	0.937
soybean curd (7.0% ptn, N×5.71)	0.051	0.176	0.175	0.305	0.269	0.081	0.091	0.195	0.193	0.186	0.302	0.121
soybean milk (3.4% ptn, N×5.71)						0.054	0.071					
vetch (28.8% ptn, N×6.25)	0.203	0.899	2.198	2.290	1.898	0.346	0.336	1.014	0.369	1.442	2.249	0.659
Common nuts and their products:												
almonds (18.6 ptn, N×5.18)	0.176	0.610	0.873	1.454	0.582	0.259	0.377	1.146	0.618	1.124	2.729	0.517
Brazil nuts (14.4% ptn, N×5.46)	0.187	0.422	0.593	1.129	0.443	0.941	0.504	0.617	0.483	0.823	2.247	0.367
cashews (18.5% ptn, N×5.30)	0.471	0.737	1.222	1.522	0.792	0.353	0.527	0.946	0.712	1.592	2.098	0.415
coconut (3.4% ptn, N×5.30)	0.033	0.129	0.180	0.269	0.152	0.071	0.062	0.174	0.101	0.212	0.486	0.069
coconut meal (20.3% ptn, N×5.30)	0.199	0.770	1.076	1.605	0.908	0.421	0.372	1.038	0.605	1.268	2.899	0.414
filberts (12.7% ptn, N×5.30)	0.211	0.415	0.853	0.939	0.417	0.139	0.165	0.537	0.434	0.934	2.171	0.288
peanuts. See Legumes.												
pecans (9.4% ptn, N×5.30)	0.138	0.389	0.553	0.773	0.435	0.153	0.216	0.564	0.316	0.525	1.185	0.273
walnuts (English or Persian) (15.0% ptn, N×5.30)	0.175	0.589	0.767	1.228	0.441	0.306	0.320	0.767	0.583	0.974	2.287	0.405
Other nuts and seeds and their products (ptn, N×5.30):												
acorns (10.4% ptn, N×5.30)	0.126	0.434	0.561	0.808	0.636	0.139	0.184	0.473		0.718	0.722	0.251
amaranth (14.6% ptn)	0.149	0.832	0.882	1.209	1.074	0.372	0.521	1.141		0.849	1.747	0.441
balsam pear seed meal (41.9% ptn)					1.265		0.142	2.609	0.617		5.914	0.917
breadnut tree, Ramon (9.6% ptn)	0.261	0.373	0.543	1.041	0.418	0.056		0.453		0.927	0.884	0.147
Chinese tallow tree (57.6% ptn)	0.837	2.174	3.510	4.347	1.587	0.924	0.696	2.847	2.011	2.404	10.031	1.587
chocolate tree, Nicaragua (38.5% ptn)	0.583	1.496	2.092	3.952	2.223	0.276		2.630		2.458	4.220	0.683
cottonseed flour and meal (42.3% ptn)	0.591	1.764	1.884	2.945	2.139	0.686	0.814	2.610	1.365	1.570	5.603	1.325
earpod tree, Guanacaste (34.1% ptn)	0.444	1.165	2.213	4.581	1.930	0.360		1.325			2.857	1.004
lead tree (24.1% ptn)	0.191	0.828	1.651	1.787	1.164	0.055		0.855		0.864	2.410	0.564
pumpkin seed (30.9% ptn)	0.560	0.933	1.737	2.437	1.411	0.577		1.749		1.679	4.810	0.711

LEGUMES; SEEDS; NUTS—Continued

safflower seed meal (42.1% ptn)	0.675	1.462	1.914	2.740	1.525	0.731	—	2.605	—	2.446	4.623	0.985
sesame:												
seed (19.3% ptn)	0.331	0.707	0.951	1.679	0.583	0.637	0.495	1.457	0.951	0.885	1.992	0.441
meal (33.4% ptn)	0.573	1.223	1.645	2.905	1.008	1.103	0.857	2.521	1.645	1.531	3.447	0.763
sunflower:												
kernel (23.0% ptn)	0.343	0.911	1.276	1.736	0.868	0.443	0.464	1.220	0.647	1.354	2.370	0.586
meal (39.5% ptn)	0.589	1.565	2.191	2.981	1.491	0.760	0.797	2.094	1.110	2.325	4.069	1.006
GRAINS AND THEIR PRODUCTS												
Barley (12.8% ptn, N×5.83)	0.160	0.433	0.545	0.889	0.433	0.184	0.257	0.661	0.466	0.643	0.659	0.239
Bread, white (4% non-fat dry milk, flour basis) (8.5% ptn, N×5.70)	0.091	0.282	0.429	0.668	0.225	0.142	0.200	0.465	0.243	0.435	0.340	0.192
Buckwheat flour:												
dark (11.7% ptn, N×6.25)	0.165	0.461	0.440	0.683	0.687	0.206	0.228	0.442	0.240	0.607	0.930	0.256
light (6.4% ptn, N×6.25)	0.090	0.252	0.241	0.374	0.376	0.113	0.125	0.242	0.131	0.332	0.509	0.140
Canihua (14.7% ptn, N×6.25)	0.118	0.706	1.000	0.851	0.882	0.263	0.162	0.529	0.294	0.677	1.162	0.367
Cereal combinations:												
corn and soy grits (18.0% ptn, N×6.25)	0.116	0.792	0.841	1.656	0.772	0.271	0.311	0.832	0.562	1.054	0.982	0.472
infant food, precooked, mixed cereals with non-fat dry milk and yeast (19.4% ptn, N×6.25)	0.118	—	—	—	0.273	0.310	0.137	0.543	0.447	—	0.447	0.233
oat-corn-rye mixture, puffed (14.5% ptn, N×5.83)	0.172	0.545	0.841	1.366	0.343	0.388	0.234	0.933	0.622	0.900	0.776	0.326
Corn, field (10.0% ptn, N×6.25)	0.061	0.398	0.462	1.296	0.288	0.186	0.130	0.454	0.611	0.510	0.352	0.206
Corn flour (7.8% ptn, N×6.25)	0.047	0.311	0.361	1.011	0.225	0.145	0.101	0.354	0.477	0.398	0.275	0.161
Corn grits (8.7% ptn, N×6.25)	0.053	0.347	0.402	1.128	0.251	0.161	0.113	0.395	0.532	0.444	0.306	0.180
Cornmeal:												
whole ground (9.2% ptn, N×6.25)	0.056	0.367	0.425	1.192	0.265	0.171	0.119	0.418	0.562	0.470	0.324	0.190
degermed (7.9% ptn, N×6.25)	0.048	0.315	0.365	1.024	0.228	0.147	0.102	0.359	0.483	0.403	0.278	0.163
Corn products:												
flakes (8.1% ptn, N×6.25)	0.052	0.275	0.306	1.047	0.154	0.135	0.152	0.354	0.283	0.386	0.231	0.226
germ (14.5% ptn, N×6.25)	0.144	0.622	0.578	1.030	0.791	0.232	0.130	0.483	0.343	0.789	1.134	0.464
gluten (10.0% ptn, N×6.25)	0.059	0.344	0.443	1.563	0.179	0.282	0.141	0.558	0.582	0.512	0.322	0.200
hominy (8.7% ptn, N×6.25)	0.084	0.316	0.349	0.810	0.358	0.099	0.030	0.333	0.331	0.398	0.444	0.203
masa (2.8% ptn, N×6.25)	0.010	—	—	—	0.103	0.108	—	—	—	—	—	—
pozol (5.9% ptn, N×6.25)	0.042	0.336	0.304	0.591	0.234	0.087	—	0.254	—	0.267	0.197	0.122
tortilla (5.8% ptn, N×6.25)	0.031	0.235	0.345	0.939	0.145	0.111	—	0.252	—	0.304	0.223	0.128

GRAINS AND PRODUCTS—Continued

Protein Content, and Nitrogen Conversion Factor	Trypto-phan (Gm.)	Threo-nine (Gm.)	Iso-leucine (Gm.)	Leucine (Gm.)	Lysine (Gm.)	Methi-onine (Gm.)	Cystine (Gm.)	Phenyl-alanine (Gm.)	Tyro-sine (Gm.)	Valine (Gm.)	Argi-nine (Gm.)	Histi-dine (Gm.)
zein (16.1% ptn, NX6.25)	0.010	0.495	0.822	3.184	—	0.281	0.162	1.664	0.981	0.654	0.286	0.216
Job's tears (13.8% ptn, NX5.83)	0.066	0.620	1.065	3.506	0.362	0.459	0.265	0.703	—	—	0.518	0.317
Millets:												
foxtail millet (9.7% ptn, NX5.83)	0.103	0.323	0.790	1.737	0.218	0.291	—	0.697	—	0.717	0.374	0.218
little millet (7.2% ptn, NX5.83)	0.047	0.262	0.517	0.841	0.138	0.178	—	0.370	—	0.471	0.363	0.147
pearl millet (11.4% ptn, NX5.83)	0.248	0.456	0.635	1.746	0.383	0.270	0.152	0.506	—	0.682	0.524	0.240
ragimillet (6.2% ptn, NX5.83)	0.085	0.270	0.398	0.620	0.202	0.270	0.187	0.263	—	0.473	0.100	0.079
Oatmeal and rolled oats (14.2% ptn, NX5.83)	0.183	0.470	0.733	1.065	0.521	0.209	0.309	0.758	0.524	0.845	0.935	0.261
Quinoa (11.0% ptn, NX6.25)	0.120	0.523	0.722	0.781	0.729	0.278	0.107	0.394	0.253	0.447	0.820	0.297
Rice:												
brown (7.5% ptn, NX5.95)	0.081	0.294	0.352	0.646	0.296	0.135	0.102	0.377	0.343	0.524	0.432	0.126
white and converted (7.6% ptn, NX5.95)	0.082	0.298	0.356	0.655	0.300	0.137	0.103	0.382	0.347	0.531	0.438	0.128
Rice products:												
flakes or puffed (5.9% ptn, NX5.95)	0.046	2.177	0.630	0.838	0.056	0.420	0.044	0.286	0.124	0.938	0.137	0.137
germ (14.2% ptn, NX5.95)	0.270	0.448	0.515	0.813	1.707	0.191	0.169	0.750	0.929	0.631	1.559	0.430
Rye (12.1% ptn, NX5.83)	0.137	—	—	—	0.494	—	0.241	0.571	0.390	—	0.591	0.276
Rye flour:												
light (9.4% ptn, NX5.83)	0.106	0.348	0.400	0.632	0.384	0.148	0.187	0.443	0.303	0.490	0.459	0.214
medium (11.4% ptn, NX5.83)	0.129	0.422	0.485	0.766	0.465	0.180	0.227	0.538	0.368	0.594	0.557	0.260
Sorghum (11.0% ptn, NX6.25)	0.123	0.394	0.598	1.767	0.299	0.190	0.183	0.547	0.303	0.628	0.417	0.211
Teosinte (22.0% ptn, NX6.25)	0.049	—	—	—	0.348	0.496	—	—	—	—	—	—
Wheat, whole grain:												
hard red spring (14.0% ptn, NX5.83)	0.173	0.403	0.607	0.939	0.384	0.214	0.307	0.691	0.523	0.648	0.670	0.286
hard red winter (12.3% ptn, NX5.83)	0.152	0.354	0.534	0.825	0.338	0.188	0.270	0.608	0.460	0.570	0.589	0.251
soft red winter (10.2% ptn, NX5.83)	0.126	0.294	0.443	0.684	0.280	0.156	0.224	0.504	0.382	0.472	0.488	0.208
white (9.4% ptn, NX5.83)	0.116	0.271	0.408	0.630	0.258	0.143	0.206	0.464	0.351	0.435	0.450	0.192
durum (12.7% ptn, NX5.83)	0.157	0.306	0.551	0.852	0.348	0.194	0.279	0.627	0.475	0.588	0.608	0.259
Wheat flour:												
whole grain (13.3% ptn, NX5.83)	0.164	0.383	0.577	0.892	0.365	0.203	0.292	0.657	0.497	0.616	0.636	0.271
intermediate extraction (12.0% ptn, NX 5.70)	—	0.392	0.619	0.924	0.356	0.198	0.320	0.732	0.335	0.583	0.549	0.286
white (10.5% ptn, NX5.70)	0.129	0.302	0.483	0.809	0.239	0.138	0.210	0.577	0.359	0.453	0.466	0.210

flour (1.6% ptn)	0.021	0.044	0.045	0.066	0.066	0.010	0.018	0.045	0.030	0.049	0.159	0.025
root (1.1% ptn)	0.014	0.030	0.031	0.045	0.045	0.007	0.012	0.031	0.021	0.033	0.110	0.017
potatoes:												
raw (2.0% ptn)	0.021	0.079	0.088	0.100	0.107	0.025	0.019	0.088	0.036	0.107	0.099	0.029
canned, solids and liquid (1.7% ptn)	0.018	0.067	0.075	0.085	0.091	0.021	0.016	0.075	0.030	0.091	0.084	0.024
flour (7.1% ptn)	0.076	0.279	0.311	0.353	0.378	0.089	0.068	0.314	0.127	0.379	0.350	0.102
sweet potatoes (Ipomaea balatas):												
raw (1.8% ptn)	0.031	0.085	0.087	0.103	0.085	0.033	0.029	0.100	0.081	0.135	0.094	0.036
dehydrated (5.0% ptn)	0.087	0.235	0.241	0.286	0.236	0.093	0.080	0.278	0.225	0.374	0.261	0.099
taro (1.9% ptn)	0.035	0.089	0.099	0.169	0.110	0.021	——	0.099	——	0.114	0.118	0.032
yam (Dioscorea spp.) (2.1% ptn)	0.035	——	——	——	0.110	0.034	——	——	——	——	——	——
Yautia malanga (1.7% ptn)	0.023	——	——	——	0.067	0.016	——	——	——	——	——	——
Other vegetables (Ptn, N×6.25):												
asparagus:												
raw (2.2% ptn)	0.027	0.066	0.080	0.096	0.103	0.032	——	0.069	——	0.106	0.123	0.036
canned, solids and liquid (1.9% ptn)	0.023	0.057	0.069	0.083	0.089	0.027	——	0.060	——	0.092	0.106	0.031
beans, snap:												
raw (2.4% ptn)	0.033	0.091	0.109	0.139	0.126	0.035	0.024	0.057	0.050	0.115	0.101	0.045
canned, solids and liquid (1.0% ptn)	0.014	0.038	0.045	0.058	0.052	0.015	0.010	0.024	0.021	0.048	0.042	0.019
beets:												
raw (1.6% ptn)	0.014	0.034	0.051	0.055	0.086	0.006	——	0.027	——	0.049	0.028	0.022
canned, solids and liquid (0.9% ptn)	0.008	0.019	0.029	0.031	0.048	0.003	——	0.015	——	0.028	0.016	0.012
broccoli (3.3% ptn)	0.037	0.122	0.126	0.163	0.147	0.050	——	0.119	——	0.170	0.192	0.063
carrots:												
raw (1.2% ptn)	0.010	0.043	0.046	0.065	0.052	0.010	0.029	0.042	0.020	0.056	0.041	0.017
canned, solids and liquid (0.5% ptn)	0.004	0.018	0.019	0.027	0.022	0.004	0.012	0.018	0.008	0.023	0.017	0.007
cauliflower (2.4% ptn)	0.033	0.102	0.104	0.162	0.134	0.047	——	0.075	0.034	0.144	0.110	0.048
celery (1.3% ptn)	0.012	——	——	——	0.021	0.015	0.006	——	0.016	——	——	——
chayote (0.6% ptn)	0.008	——	——	——	0.038	0.001	——	——	——	——	——	——
cowpeas, yardlong, immature pod (3.4% ptn)	0.034	——	——	——	0.203	0.021	——	——	——	——	——	——
cucumbers (0.7% ptn)	0.005	0.019	0.022	0.030	0.031	0.007	——	0.016	——	0.024	0.053	0.001
cushaw (1.5% ptn)	0.014	——	——	——	0.044	0.008	——	——	——	——	——	——
eggplant (1.1% ptn)	0.010	0.038	0.056	0.068	0.030	0.006	——	0.048	——	0.065	0.037	0.019
mallow (3.7% ptn)	0.144	0.155	——	0.259	0.155	0.030	——	0.166	——	0.181	0.189	0.063
mushrooms:												

Protein Content, and Nitrogen Conversion Factor	Trypto-phan (Gm.)	Threo-nine (Gm.)	Iso-leucine (Gm.)	Leucine (Gm.)	Lysine (Gm.)	Methi-onine (Gm.)	Cystine (Gm.)	Phenyl-alanine (Gm.)	Tyro-sine (Gm.)	Valine (Gm.)	Argi-nine (Gm.)	Histi-dine (Gm.)
VEGETABLES—Continued												
(Agaricus campestris)*	0.006	---	0.532	0.281	0.088	0.167	---	0.018	---	0.378	0.235	0.027
(Lactarius spp.)†	0.006	0.156	0.201	0.139	0.076	0.021	0.017	0.065	0.079	0.116	0.021	0.030
okra (1.8% ptn)	0.018	0.066	0.069	0.101	0.064	0.022	---	0.039	0.046	0.091	0.093	0.014
onions, mature (1.4% ptn)	0.021	0.022	0.021	0.037	0.044	0.013	---	0.059	---	0.031	0.180	---
peppers (1.2% ptn)	0.009	0.050	0.046	0.057	0.058	0.008	---	0.032	---	0.041	0.032	0.016
prickly pears (1.1% ptn)	0.009	0.053	0.044	0.063	0.034	0.011	---	---	---	0.045	0.043	0.019
pumpkin (1.2% ptn)	0.016	0.028	0.044	---	---	0.002	---	---	---	0.030	---	---
radishes (1.2% ptn)	0.005	0.059	---	---	---	---	---	---	0.016	---	---	---
seepweed (2.6% ptn)	0.027	0.089	0.113	0.152	0.089	0.013	---	0.116	---	0.091	0.062	0.036
soybean sprouts (6.2% ptn)	---	0.159	0.225	0.265	0.211	0.045	---	0.186	---	0.225	0.225	0.133
squash, summer (0.6% ptn)	0.005	0.014	0.019	0.027	0.023	0.008	---	0.016	---	0.022	0.027	0.009
tomatoes and cherry tomatoes (1.0% ptn)	0.009	0.033	0.029	0.041	0.042	0.007	---	0.028	0.014	0.028	0.029	0.015
turnips (1.1% ptn)	---	---	---	---	0.057	0.012	---	0.020	0.029	---	---	---
waxgourd, Chinese (0.4% ptn)	0.002	---	---	---	0.009	0.003	---	---	---	---	---	---
MISCELLANEOUS FOOD ITEMS												
Vegetable patty or steak (principally wheat ptn) (15% ptn, N×5.70)	0.142	0.411	0.884	1.079	0.321	0.253	---	0.811	0.580	0.705	0.597	0.321
Yeast:												
baker's, compressed‡ (N×6.25)	0.122	0.655	0.655	1.151	0.914	0.248	0.120	0.607	---	0.840	0.536	0.353
brewer's, dried§ (N×6.25)	0.710	2.353	2.398	3.226	3.300	0.836	0.548	1.902	1.902	2.723	2.250	1.251
primary, dried:												
(Saccharomyces cerevisiae)§ (N×6.25)	0.636	2.353	2.708	3.300	3.337	0.851	0.444	1.813	2.472	2.553	1.931	1.103
(Torulopsis utilis)§ (N×6.25)	0.636	2.331	3.323	3.707	3.648	0.710	0.422	2.361	2.464	2.901	3.337	1.251

*Total nitrogen is 0.58%. This is equivalent to 2.4% protein on the basis that two-thirds of the nitrogen is protein nitrogen. If total nitrogen is used for the calculation, the protein content is 3.6%.

†Total nitrogen is 0.60%. This is equivalent to 2.9% protein on the basis that two-thirds of the nitrogen is protein nitrogen. If total nitrogen is used for the calculation, the protein content is 4.3%.

‡Total nitrogen is 2.1%. This is equivalent to 10.6% protein on the basis that four-fifths of the nitrogen is protein nitrogen. If total nitrogen is used for the calculation, the protein content is 13.1%.

§Total nitrogen is 7.4%. This is equivalent to 36.9% protein on the basis that four-fifths of the nitrogen is protein nitrogen. If total nitrogen is used for the calculation, the protein content is 46.1%.

MINERAL ELEMENTS* AND EXCESS OF ACIDITY OR ALKALINITY†
PER 100 GM. OF FOODS, EDIBLE PORTION

| Food | Minerals | | | | | | Excess‡ | |
	Mag-nesium (Gm.)	Potas-sium (Gm.)	Sodium (Gm.)	Chlo-rine (Gm.)	Sul-phur (Gm.)		Acidity (Cc. of N Acid HCl)	Alkalinity (Cc. of N Alkali NaOH)
Almonds	0.275	0.756	0.024	0.037	0.164		2.2	12.0–18.3
Apples:								
fresh	0.006	0.116	0.015	0.004	0.004		....	0.8–3.7
dried	0.029	0.557	0.072	0.019	0.019		....	....
Apricots:								
fresh	0.012	0.370	0.021	0.004	0.006		....	4.8–8.4
dried	0.062	1.024	0.100	0.021	0.031		....	31.3–41.9
Asparagus	0.015	0.200	0.008	0.047	0.051		1.0	0.8
Bananas	0.024	0.412	0.023	0.163	0.013		....	4.4–7.9
Barley, entire	0.126	0.495	0.070	0.139	0.153		6.0–17.5	....

*W. H. Peterson, J. T. Skinner, and F. M. Strong, *Elements of food biochemistry* (New York: Prentice-Hall, Inc., 1944), pp. 262–65.

†M. A. Bridges and M. R. Mattice, *Food and beverage analyses* (Philadelphia: Lea & Febiger, 1942), pp. 200–214.

‡The ranges indicated come from reports of several authors, in which variety and method of preparation influence the results in part. For individual studies and sources of data see Bridges and Mattice, *op. cit.*

Food	Minerals					Excess‡	
	Magnesium (Gm.)	Potassium (Gm.)	Sodium (Gm.)	Chlorine (Gm.)	Sulphur (Gm.)	Acidity (Cc. of N Acid HCl)	Alkalinity (Cc. of N Alkali NaOH)
Beans:							
dried	0.165	1.284	0.189	0.007	0.224	....	18.0–23.9
Lima, fresh	0.067	0.606	0.089	0.009	0.068	....	14.0
dried	0.181	1.899	0.282	0.025	0.156	....	41.6
string or green	0.032	0.288	0.012	0.045	0.024	....	4.1–5.4
Beef	0.032	0.382	0.066	0.056	0.221	8.1–38.5	....
Beets	0.027	0.235	0.040	0.040	0.017	....	8.9–11.4
Beet greens	0.097	0.390	....	....	0.035	....	....
Brains	0.016	0.269	0.160	0.155	0.130	17.7–20.7	....
Bread, white	0.034	0.110	0.517	0.602	0.083	1.5–7.1	....
Broccoli	0.024	0.352	0.030	0.076	0.126	....	3.6–4.9
Brussels sprouts	0.015	0.375	....	....	....	....	....
Butter	0.002	0.019	§	§	0.009	0.4–4.3	....
Cabbage:	0.016	0.217	0.038	0.034	0.074	....	1.4–8.2
celery	0.011	0.400	0.028	0.023	0.013	....	....
Cantaloupe	0.016	0.243	0.048	0.048	0.016	....	7.5
Carrots	0.020	0.219	0.050	0.035	0.019	....	4.4–10.8
Cauliflower	0.023	0.292	0.048	0.038	0.074	....	1.4–5.3

§Variable.　　‡Partly acid in ripe.

Celery	0.025	0.320	0.101	0.225	0.021	....	2.5–11.1
Cheese, hard	0.031	0.116	0.900	0.972	0.214	0.3–11.8	3.6–5.1
Cherries	0.012	0.125	0.015	0.004	0.018	....	1.7–7.3
Chestnuts	0.048	0.415	0.037	0.010	0.049	9.6–25.4	7.4–11.3
Chicken	0.047	0.402	0.054	0.034	0.303		....
Chocolate	0.082	0.400	0.019	0.009	0.114	8.1	7.9
Cocoa	0.192	0.534	0.060	0.050	0.197		0.7
Coconut, fresh	0.040	0.360	0.040	0.120	0.044	....	4.1–7.0
Collards	0.017	....	....	....	....	....	....
Corn:							
field, mature	0.142	0.300	0.110	0.041	0.124	....	....
sweet							
fresh	0.047	0.278	0.148	0.050	0.037	1.8	....
mature	0.121	0.415	0.036	0.019	0.146	6.0	....
Cowpeas, dried	0.265	1.305	0.366	0.019	0.250		....
Crabs	0.117	0.271	0.366	0.570	0.255	39.5	....
Cranberries	0.005	0.056	0.002	0.004	0.008	....	3.2
Cream	0.000	0.112	0.031	0.067	0.033	....	0.4–3.2
Cucumbers	0.020	0.170	0.026	0.028	0.011	....	3.2–31.5
Currants:							
fresh	0.031	0.208	0.015	0.010	0.021	....	0.7–8.8
dried	0.155	1.040	0.075	0.050	0.105	....	5.8–21.8
Dates	0.065	0.580	0.040	0.253	0.048	....	5.5–12.4

| | MINERALS | | | | | EXCESS‡ | |
Food	Magnesium (Gm.)	Potassium (Gm.)	Sodium (Gm.)	Chlorine (Gm.)	Sulphur (Gm.)	Acidity (Cc. of N Acid HCl)	Alkalinity (Cc. of N Alkali NaOH)
Eel	0.018	0.241	0.032	0.035	0.133	7.0–9.9	....
Eggplant	0.015	0.260	0.026	0.063	0.020	....	4.5
Eggs	0.009	0.149	0.111	0.100	0.233	11.1–24.5	....
Egg white	0.011	0.149	0.175	0.131	0.211	4.8–8.3	....
Egg yolk	0.013	0.110	0.078	0.067	0.214	25.3–51.8	....
Figs:							
fresh	0.020	0.205	0.043	0.037	0.017	....	10.0–100.9
dried	0.068	0.709	0.151	0.126	0.060	....	....
Fish (all kinds)	0.024	0.375	0.064	0.137	0.199	8.5–20.1	....
Flour, wheat, white	0.021	0.137	0.053	0.079	0.155	7.4–9.6	....
Frog	0.024	0.308	0.055	0.040	0.163	10.6–15.8	....
Garlic	0.008	0.130	0.009	0.004	0.318	....	....
Goose	0.031	0.406	....	0.009	0.326	7.7–24.5	....
Gooseberries	0.009	0.150	0.010	0.009	0.015	....	2.1–7.6
Grapefruit	0.007	0.164	0.006	0.007	0.005	....	6.4
Grapes	0.004	0.267	0.011	0.002	0.009	....	2.7–7.2
Haddock	0.017	0.334	0.099	0.241	0.225	8.5–19.7	....
Heart	0.035	0.329	0.102	0.204	0.151	27.6	....
Honey	0.004	0.051	0.006	0.015	0.003	1.1	0.4–4.6

Horse-radish	0.028	0.550	0.094	0.013	0.234		2.7–5.8
Kale	0.055	0.486	0.050	0.120	0.160		4.0–17.0
Kidney	0.019	0.240	0.238	0.376	0.148	8.4–31.0	
Kohlrabi	0.052	0.370	0.050	0.050	0.039		6.0
Lamb (see Mutton)							
Leeks	0.037	0.380	0.036	0.110	0.056		5.5–11.3
Lemons	0.006	0.152	0.009	0.006	0.012		5.5–9.9
Lentils, dried	0.082	0.662	0.754	0.062	0.123	5.2–17.8	0.4–2.0
Lettuce	0.015	0.256	0.028	0.085	0.014		3.8–14.1
Liver	0.021	0.255	0.021	0.091	0.258	9.4–49.5	
Lobster	0.022	0.258				38.4	
Macaroni, dry	0.038	0.054	0.010	0.077	0.119	3.8–9.6	
Milk:							
cow							
fresh	0.019	0.129	0.047	0.114	0.031		1.8–4.2
evaporated	0.038	0.258	0.094	0.228	0.067		4.6
powder	0.118	0.955	0.348	1.029	0.229		21.6
goat	0.005	0.055	0.026	0.163			
human	0.012	0.280	0.013	0.058	0.142		1.8–4.0
Mushrooms			0.013	0.026	0.025		
Mustard greens	0.016	0.330	0.020	0.090	0.142		
Mutton	0.033	0.260	0.070	0.069	0.187	4.5–22.5	
Oatmeal (rolled oats)	0.143	0.365	0.072	0.027	0.207	1.5–13.2	

Food	Minerals					Excess‡	
	Magnesium (Gm.)	Potassium (Gm.)	Sodium (Gm.)	Chlorine (Gm.)	Sulphur (Gm.)	Acidity (Cc. of N Acid HCl)	Alkalinity (Cc. of N Alkali NaOH)
Oats, entire	0.150	0.450	0.168	0.089	0.187	....	....
Onions	0.016	0.200	0.020	0.053	0.065	....	0.2–8.4
Orange juice	0.014	0.200	0.006	0.008	0.005	....	4.5
Oranges	0.011	0.177	0.014	0.006	0.011	....	5.6–9.6
Parsnips	0.038	0.396	0.010	0.038	0.025	....	6.6–11.9
Peaches:							
fresh	0.015	0.174	0.012	0.006	0.005	....	3.8–6.1
dried	0.087	1.009	0.070	0.035	0.029	....	4.1–12.1
Peanuts	0.169	0.706	0.052	0.040	0.276	3.9–16.4	....
Pears	0.005	0.110	0.010	0.004	0.010	....	1.5–3.6
Peas:							
green	0.035	0.259	0.024	0.049	0.035	1.4–2.9	1.2–5.2
mature	0.121	0.943	0.072	0.034	0.178	0.5–3.4	1.2–10.3
Peppers:							
green	0.025	0.270	0.015	0.031	0.030	....	....
red	0.013	0.120	0.006	0.014	0.030	....	....
Persimmons	0.005	0.170	0.013	0.009	0.011	....	....
Pike	0.031	0.416	0.029	0.032	0.218	2.8–19.5	....
Pineapple	0.014	0.230	0.008	0.038	0.003	....	2.2–7.00

Plums	0.010	0.212	0.003	0.002	0.004	……	4.8
Pork	0.027	0.415	0.081	0.040	0.216	7.7–28.6	……
Potatoes	0.027	0.498	0.030	0.048	0.033	……	7.0–12.8
Prunes, dried	0.032	0.845	0.101	0.004	0.024	……	7.8–20.3
Pumpkins	0.021	0.198	0.011	0.025	0.016	……	0.3–7.8
Rabbit	0.029	0.415	0.047	0.051	0.184	14.8–22.4	……
Radishes	0.014	0.166	0.083	0.056	0.038	……	2.9–7.2
Raisins	0.017	0.796	0.120	0.068	0.043	……	23.7–27.0
Raspberries	0.018	0.141	0.007	0.010	0.012	……	4.1–6.1
Rhubarb	0.015	0.392	0.010	0.070	0.008	……	8.6–13.0
Rice:							
entire	0.141	0.334	0.068	0.066	0.121	……	……
polished	0.033	0.046	0.012	0.056	0.114	2.5–9.0	……
Rutabagas	0.015	0.210	0.052	0.031	0.069	……	8.5
Rye, entire	0.136	0.477	0.060	0.043	0.152	11.3	……
Sardines, fresh	0.035	……	……	……	……	11.4–26.5	……
Shrimps:							
dried	……	……	……	……	……	……	……
salted	0.327	0.760	§	§	0.183	……	……
Soybeans, mature	0.287	1.693	0.280	0.007	0.269	1.6	……
Spaghetti (*see Maca-roni*)							
Spinach	0.048	0.416	0.093	0.118	0.027	……	5.1–39.6

Food	Minerals					Excess‡	
	Magnesium (Gm.)	Potassium (Gm.)	Sodium (Gm.)	Chlorine (Gm.)	Sulphur (Gm.)	Acidity (Cc. of N Acid HCl)	Alkalinity (Cc. of N Alkali NaOH)
Squash	0.006	0.161	0.011	0.018	0.029	....	2.8
Strawberries	0.019	0.205	....	0.013	0.013	....	1.8–3.5
Sugar beets	0.041	0.440	0.130	0.180	0.021	....	3.3–9.4
Sweet potatoes	0.035	0.381	0.031	0.022	0.014	....	5.0–7.9
Tomatoes	0.016	0.277	0.013	0.048	0.017	10.4–19.5	5.6–13.7
Turkey	0.028	0.367	0.130	0.123	0.234	....	....
Turnip greens	0.079	0.300	0.260	0.390	0.051	....	2.3
Turnips	0.019	0.193	0.104	0.054	0.048	....	2.7–10.2
Veal	0.030	0.380	0.086	0.073	0.199	9.8–28.5	....
Venison	0.029	0.336	0.070	0.041	0.211	23.8	....
Walnuts	0.132	0.606	0.013	0.030	0.120	7.9–9.2	....
Watercress	0.010	0.100	0.031	0.059	0.071	....	1.8–2.7
Watermelon	0.006	0.071	0.012	0.006	0.005	....	....
Wheat:							
entire	0.163	0.409	0.106	0.088	0.175	9.7–12.0	....
bran	0.420	1.252	0.007	0.042	0.245	....	....
Yams	0.015	0.290	0.015	0.037	0.013	....	....

172

BIBLIOGRAPHY

Title	Author	Publisher
About Biochemistry	Esther Chapman	Thorsons Publishers Ltd.
About Food Values	Barbara Davis	Thorsons Publishers Ltd.
About Rice and Lentils	Harvey Day	Thorsons Publishers Ltd.
The Acid-Alkaline Balance	Mira Louise	New Horizons Publishers
Basic Nutrition and Cell Nutrition	R. F. Milton, Ph.D.	Provoker Press
The Complete Book of Food and Nutrition		
The Complete Handbook of Nutrition	J. I. Rodale and Staff	Rodale Books Inc.
Diet For a Small Planet	Steve and Gary Null	Robert Speller & Sons Inc.
Food Combining Made Easy	Frances Moore Lappe	Ballentine Books
Handbook of Diet Therapy	Herbert M. Shelton	Dr. Shelton's Health School
The Hygienic Way of Life;	Dorothea Turner	University of Chicago Press
The Argument for Vegetarianism		
Let's Eat Right to Keep Fit	Hereward Carrington, Ph.D.	Health Research Series Publications
Man and Food	Adelle Davis	New American Library
Nerves and Muscles	Magnus Pyke	McGraw-Hill Book Company
Nutrition and Your Mind	Robert Galambos	Anchor Books
Nutrition in a Nutshell	George Watson	
The Oxford Book of Plant Foods	Roger J. Williams	Dolphin Books
	Masefield, Wallis, Harrison, Nicholson	Oxford University Press
Proteins as Human Food	R. A. Lawrie	Avi Publishing Company
Protein, Building Blocks of Life	Bob Hoffman	York Barbell Company
Protein for Muscle-Bone-Skin	Dr. Bernard Jensen	Author

173

If you require further information concerning any material presented in this book (i.e references, statistics, clinical observations, or biographical sources), write to the Nutrition Institute of America, Inc., 200 West 86th Street, #17A, New York, New York, 10024.

ON SALE WHEREVER PAPERBACKS ARE SOLD — or
use this coupon to order directly from the publisher.

HEALTH & NUTRITION
Books to help you feel better, live longer and get more out of life . . .

(All books listed are paperback editions unless otherwise noted.)

Please send me:

_____ CHOLESTEROL COUNTER Elizabeth Weiss & Rita Wolfson P3208-$1.00

_____ ACUPUNCTURE Marc Duke A3156 $1.50

_____ ALLERGIES: What They Are and What to Do About Them J. Rudolph, M.D. V3101 $1.25

_____ BETTER EYESIGHT WITHOUT GLASSES W.H. Bates V2332-$1.25

_____ CORONARIES, CHOLESTEROL & CHLORINE J.M. Price, M.D. N2544-95¢

_____ EAT WELL TO KEEP WELL Dr. Max Warmbrand N2173-95¢

_____ HOW TO LIVE WITH DIABETES H. Dolger, M.D. N2353-95¢

_____ HEART ATTACK: ARE YOU A CANDIDATE? A. Blumenfeld N2433-95¢

_____ IF YOU MUST SMOKE J.I. Rodale N1881-95¢

_____ LIVING WITHOUT PAIN Dr. Max Warmbrand N2477-95¢

_____ THE POISONS IN YOUR FOOD Wm. Longgood V2043-$1.25

_____ SECRETS OF HEALTH & BEAUTY Linda Clark N2350-95¢

_____ STAY YOUNG LONGER Linda Clark N1745-95¢

_____ PICTORIAL ENCYCLOPEDIA OF EXERCISE FOR HEALTH AND THERAPY E. Flatto, N.D. J3098-$3.95

_____ THE ENCLYCOPEDIA OF NATURAL HEALTH Max Warmbrand, M.D. 9226-$4.95 (hardcover)

_____ THE NATURAL FOODS COOKBOOK Beatrice Trum Hunter V1589-$1.25

_____ ADVENTURES IN COOKING WITH HEALTH FOODS N. Sutton N2514-95¢

_____ ALLERGY COOKING M.L. Conrad N1914-95¢

_____ VITAMIN E FOR AILING AND HEALTHY HEARTS Wilfred E. Shute, M.D. & Harald Taub H2744-$1.65

_____ VITAMIN E AND AGING Erwin Di Cyan, Ph.D. V2761-$1.25

Send to PYRAMID PUBLICATIONS,
Dept. M.O., 9 Garden Street, Moonachie, N.J. 07074

NAME _____

ADDRESS _____

CITY _____

STATE _____ ZIP _____

Enclosed $_____ payment in full, including 25¢ per book shipping charge if order is under $5.00. Orders over $5.00 are shipped free. No COD's or stamps. Please allow three to four weeks for delivery. Prices subject to change.   P-3